After Vietnam

After Vietnam

Legacies of a Lost War

■

EDITED BY CHARLES E. NEU

The Johns Hopkins University Press

Baltimore and London

This book has been brought to publication with the generous assistance of the Albert Shaw Memorial Lectures at the Johns Hopkins University.

Printed in the United States of America on acid-free paper
9 8 7 6 5 4 3 2

The Johns Hopkins University Press
2715 North Charles Street
Baltimore, Maryland 21218-4363
www.press.jhu.edu

Library of Congress Cataloging-in-Publication Data will be found at the end of this book.
A catalog record for this book is available from the British Library.

ISBN 0-8018-6327-9
ISBN 0-8018-6332-5 (pbk.)

Contents

Foreword

How quickly we forget. The cover of the *New York Times* magazine section recently featured a large fist painted like the American flag (March 28, 1999). "What the World Needs Now," the lead article said, is for the United States no longer to be "afraid to act like the almighty superpower that it is." Thomas L. Friedman, the paper's foreign affairs columnist, urged the country to promote a global plan that would include a mixture of "neoliberal macroeconomics" and U.S.-style "regulatory institutions and laws": "managing globalization," Friedman argued, "is a role from which America dare not shrink." The "benign superpower" must, he said, provide the "hidden fist" without which the "hidden hand of the market will never work."

Does that sound familiar? It does to me. It's an echo of what I heard from the "best and brightest" in the 1960s as the United States entered the struggle in Vietnam. An intricate blend of hubris, liberal enthusiasm, ethnocentrism, and naiveté, this confident ideology at first appealed to me. I had served in the U.S. Navy during the Korean War, and I still was convinced that President Eisenhower's strategy for fighting the Cold War against communism should be the central theme of our foreign policy. During the early 1960s, I had a Yale Ph.D. in hand and had completed a year of postdoctoral training at the Harvard Business School. I was an assistant professor of history at Rice University and, like most teachers in that capacity, was in effect trying to complete my higher education. I still had much to learn.

In the years that followed, the war in Southeast Asia accelerated my education, teaching me a great deal about America's political institutions and the limits of American power. By the 1970s, then at the Johns Hopkins University, I demonstrated in Washington, D.C., against the bombing of Cambodia and the continuation of U.S. military involvement in Vietnam. At last I understood why all of our previous military interventions had failed to redirect revolutionary movements in Mexico, Russia, and China, among others.

In the years that followed our defeat in Vietnam, I've watched with interest as new generations have emerged and new attitudes about the exercise of power have become popular. Vietnam receded. The war in Southeast Asia finally became something that my students said their parents talked about, something that interested students largely because it had played such a powerful role in the lives of their mothers and fathers. For the students themselves, however, the Vietnam War engaged emotions no more than did the other wars described in their textbooks—no more than World Wars I or II or, for that matter, the Spanish-American War. They were slogans, manifestos, numbers, dates, and places, most of which they couldn't remember once they had passed the final exam.

Reflecting on that process—something we might call "historical forgetting," the flip side of the trendy idea of "historical memory"—I convinced the History Department at Johns Hopkins to sponsor a symposium, "Legacies of a Lost War." With the support of Chairman John Russell-Wood, we organized the Albert Shaw Memorial Lectures around this theme. The series gave us a platform and a budget, and Professor Charles E. Neu of Brown University kindly agreed to put together a program that would explore the transitions that have taken place since 1975 in the impacts of that national experience on the political, intellectual, military, and cultural realms. He wisely decided to include the war's historical legacy for Vietnam as well as for the superpower it defeated. We agreed that it would also be instructive to include an insightful essay by one of the leading participants in the American war effort, former Secretary of Defense Robert McNamara.

Do we have a purpose other than writing scholarly histories? Unable ourselves to forget, do we want to remind a new generation of how much America once paid to learn that it could not reshape the world in its own image by using military power? I cannot speak for all of the contributors, but my own answer is "Yes, of course!" Fearful of the fist and certain that American solutions to national and international problems will not always have universal appeal, I was eager to trace the path that led Americans from the slough of defeat in the 1970s to the exuberance of the late 1990s. I thought it would also be instructive for Americans to read about the legacy of victory in a Vietnamese nation that has been less successful in peace than it was in war. Understanding these threads of twentieth-century history, we will perhaps be more prudent in our exercise of military power. Judging by recent events in Serbia, we are today loaded with pride and short of prudence, just as we were in the early 1960s.

Louis Galambos
Professor of History
Editor, The Papers of Dwight David Eisenhower
The Johns Hopkins University

Introduction

On many levels and in many different ways, the process of coming to terms with the Vietnam War continues to unfold. As Morley Safer writes, each witness to that conflict is "still imprisoned, to one extent or another, by that place and that time."[1] Memories of the war remain vivid among many Americans, who are still trying to understand why we fought so long and so hard in such a distant place, and why, in the end, we and our allies in Saigon suffered such a humiliating defeat. And many Americans remain reluctant to accept the outcome of the war, especially the communist regime that triumphed in the spring of 1975—the Socialist Republic of Vietnam. Not until February 1994, nineteen years after the fall of Saigon, did the United States finally lift its economic embargo against Vietnam; the next year the two nations established full diplomatic relations. But the new American ambassador, Pete Peterson, a former Air Force pilot who was shot down over North Vietnam and held as a POW for six and a half years, did not arrive in Hanoi until May 1997. Peterson's appointment signified that, at least at the governmental level, the two nations were willing to put the past behind them and look toward what the new ambassador termed a "bright and promising future."[2]

More than a year later, in August 1998, the change in American-Vietnamese relations was highlighted in a different way with the demolition of the former American embassy in Ho Chi Minh City. The U.S. government, having regained possession of the building, decided to tear it down and construct a new, more modest consular edifice. The once impressive embassy, with its honeycombed concrete walls, rooftop helicopter pad, and fortress-like compound, had been a symbol of American power after its completion in 1967. In the final days of the war, with crowds of Vietnamese clamoring at its gates and helicopters lifting the final evacuees from its rooftop, it became the setting for the chaotic American departure from South Vietnam. For millions of Americans watching the collapse of that nation, the American embassy building and its compound formed the last of a series of striking visual images produced by the war. The demolition of this building, which embodied so many hopes and bitter memories, signified, like Ambassador Peterson's appointment, the dawn of a new era in the relations between the two nations.

As the two governments now focus on mundane tasks, such as the negotiation of a trade agreement, they do so in an atmosphere that remains emotionally charged. On the American side, many questions about the conduct of the war remain unanswered; the titles of some recent books, such as *Dereliction of Duty, The Color of Truth, A Tangled Web,* and *A Better War,*[3] reflect the intensity of the quest for greater insight into why the war was fought and how it was lost. And some Vietnam veterans still seek to understand their sacrifices and to put the war behind them. In 1993 Harold G. Moore, who led a battalion in the bloody battle of the Ia Drang Valley in November 1965, returned to Vietnam to meet with former enemy commanders and revisit Landing Zone X-Ray. Moore and other veterans of that campaign walked around the battle site and paid a moving tribute to comrades they had left behind. As the survivors stood in a circle on that "sacred spot," arms across the shoulders of those on either side, Moore remarked, "Once again we're back with our dear brothers, God rest their souls."[4]

Evidence of the legacy of the war in American life is everywhere, revealed in the anguish of some Vietnam veterans, in the persistence of MIA-POW flags, in the presence of one million Indochinese immigrants in America, in the production of movies and television specials dealing with the war, in the way in which the war still lingers in our national politics and foreign policy decisions, in the enormous popularity of the Vietnam Veterans Memorial in Washington, D.C. In contrast to other monuments in that city, tokens of remembrance—notes, old dog tags, flags—are left beneath the polished black granite slabs by those who still feel the pain of the war.

The impact of the war on America was so great that efforts to understand its consequences began soon after it ended, and have continued all the way to the present. This volume is a part of this larger enterprise to sort through the residue of the war. While earlier works have often been diffuse, covering a wide range of topics, these essays take a different approach. Four distinguished scholars focus on well-defined aspects of the war's legacy, while one of the major architects of the war contributes a final chapter pondering foreign policy issues of the twenty-first century. The result is a volume that deepens our understanding of particular aspects of the war's aftermath in both America and Vietnam. We realize, however, that these essays leave many questions unanswered, and that they are part of a complicated, long-term historical process of exploring the war and its legacy.

Students of the Vietnam War often state that its greatest long-term impact in the United States was in the realm of the spirit. The collapse of South Vietnam, they claim, brought a loss of American innocence or an end of American exceptionalism. My essay accepts this generalization as a starting point, but also moves beyond it to analyze how the Vietnam War helped to change Americans' sense of themselves, or the "mental landscape of the nation." If the Vietnam War served as a great divide, separating the World War II generation from the Vietnam generation, it is essential to understand the point of view of this older generation and how the war in Vietnam defied the expectations of both those who stayed at home and those who fought in South Vietnam. As the Vietnam War challenged widely held national myths, it brought frustration and disillusionment and, most important, a weakening of Americans' sense of their past and of their vision of the future. Americans had responded to the war in Vietnam with an almost reflexive patriotism, willing to trust the judgments of their leaders and to answer their call for service in a distant war. Well before the end of the war, however, the trust of most Americans in their leaders had eroded, and many young people challenged the wisdom of the war and sought ways to avoid serving in it. The nation that entered the Vietnam War was far different from the one that left it. If we are to understand the legacy of the war in its broadest sense, we must trace this far-ranging transformation in our identity as a nation.

The Vietnam War was one of a series of upheavals in America during the 1960s that have given that decade a special significance in recent American history. In his contribution to this volume, Brian Balogh seeks to put the war in historical context and to counter the tendency to blame much of what has gone wrong in American life since then on the nation's involvement in Vietnam. Vietnam became such a powerful metaphor for turmoil and decline that it obscured, both at the time and later, other forces that contributed to fundamental changes in America. The Vietnam War, Balogh argues, was not primarily responsible for the decline of authority, or the higher level of conflict in American society, or the fragmentation of national identity. Other powerful forces, such as the civil rights movement, the erosion of the authority of experts and their institutions, the pressures of the world economy on America's aging industrial base, and the end of the Cold War, were all important in reshaping the nation. Balogh reminds us of the complexity of the whole process of historical change; changes commonly viewed as benign can bring loss as well as gain. The end of the Cold War in 1990, for example, removed a heavy burden on the resources of the nation. But the Cold War had also served, for more than forty years, as a unifying force against a dangerous enemy and as a major organizing principle for the life of the nation. Its sudden end, along with the collapse of the Soviet Union, brought disorientation as well as relief, for in the absence of a major enemy abroad, Americans had to rethink their priorities and purpose as a nation.

The Vietnam War had a powerful effect on key institutions of the U.S. government—the presidency, Congress, the CIA, and, most of all, the military. In the aftermath of the fall of Saigon, most Americans pushed the war aside, avoiding coming to terms with the causes of the nation's failure. As George C. Herring points out in his essay, the American military in general, and the army in particular, could not indulge in this sort of avoidance. Disturbed by the breakdown of the army during the final years of the war and shocked by the fall of Saigon, military leaders entered the post-Vietnam years with a sense of urgency, determined to impose far-reaching reforms on the nation's armed forces. They integrated the reserves far more closely with regular forces, rethought war-fighting doctrines, devised more-realistic training techniques, developed a new generation of weaponry, and, now skeptical of civilian leadership, became far more cautious about the use of military force as an instrument of American foreign policy. The Persian Gulf War, Herring notes, was for the American military "more about Vietnam than about Kuwait," for American commanders were seeking vindication, to prove that they had learned from their failures in Vietnam and that this time they could win a swift, decisive victory.

The stunning success of the Persian Gulf War may, however, have been misleading. In the post–Cold War world, it seemed unlikely that the nation would fight in a conflict similar to the Gulf War in the foreseeable future. Rather, the end of the Cold War brought a new kind of instability in many parts of the world and with it more conflicts of the sort that erupted in what was once Yugoslavia. The American military was poorly prepared for this low-intensity warfare and reluctant to undertake it. Moreover, the transformation of the American military solved some old problems but also revealed new ones. The all-volunteer military, instituted in

1973, swept away the issues surrounding the draft but also created a group of professional soldiers isolated from civilian society. And the end of any serious external threat further increased the indifference of most Americans to military issues, causing what Herring terms a "widening gap" between military and civilian leaders that has troublesome implications for the future.

In the years after 1975, Americans traveling to Vietnam were generally impressed with how successfully the Vietnamese people had put the war behind them. Despite the loss of somewhere between one and a half and three million Vietnamese civilians and soldiers and enormous physical destruction, it seemed as if most Vietnamese had forgiven their former enemy and were oriented more toward the future than the past. The journalist Neil Sheehan, when he returned to Vietnam in 1989, was surprised by how the people had transcended the suffering of the war. While standing by the side of the road near a village in North Vietnam, waiting for his car's tire to be fixed, he watched a peasant on a bike pedal toward him. Stopping in surprise when he saw a foreigner, the peasant asked Sheehan if he was a Russian. When Sheehan replied that he was an American, the man said "good, Americans are good," and proudly stated, "I'm a veteran. I fought in the South." When Sheehan found out the area in which he had fought, he remarked that the fighting had been bitter there. "Yes," came the reply, "so many bombs, so many shells, so much napalm my hair turned gray like this." He then shook the journalist's hand, expressed a wish for peace, and pedaled away.[5]

Sheehan's encounter, like those of so many of the Americans who returned to Vietnam, was misleading, one more indication of how difficult it was for Americans, both during the war and after it was over, to see beneath the surface of Vietnamese culture and society. As Robert K. Brigham reveals in his pathbreaking essay in this volume, the war had a profound, lasting impact on the Vietnamese people and on their political culture and institutions. Communist revolutionaries had been successful in part because of their skill in linking Vietnam's past to their vision of its future, and they had fashioned a collective leadership that shared common historical experiences and that gave their cause a remarkable continuity. Their political and military strategy in the war against the United States had been brilliant. But the very qualities that brought success on the battlefield left them poorly prepared to deal with the unique problems of peace, with the unification and rebuilding of their nation after 1975. In the aftermath of this great triumph, Vietnam descended into an economic, moral, and political crisis. As aging revolutionaries mismanaged the nation, lost touch with a younger generation that had no memories of the war, and found the legitimacy of their rule challenged by Buddhist religious leaders, they relied increasingly on the myth of "revolutionary heroism" to justify the Communist Party's monopoly on political power. The war, with all its suffering and loss, could only be remembered as glorious, not tragic.

Party leaders also found their version of the past challenged by novelists who had fought in the south. Duong Thu Huong's *Paradise of the Blind* (1988) and *Novel without a Name* (1995) and Bao Ninh's *The Sorrow of War* (1991) questioned the official war story, portraying a grim, merciless struggle that left them and many other members of their generation disenchanted with the nation's grand cause. In America the Vietnam War destroyed old myths and brought a new era of disillusionment; it may be that in Vietnam, as well, the war brought a sea change that is only now coming into view.

Robert S. McNamara approaches the Vietnam War from a different perspective than that of the other contributors to this volume. As Secretary of Defense from January 1961 to February 1968, he was an influential adviser of John F. Kennedy and Lyndon B. Johnson and a major architect of the Vietnam War. Initially McNamara was an advocate of escalation, convinced that the geopolitical stakes in South Vietnam were great and that American military intervention would break the will of the enemy and lead to an acceptable political solution. He was an extraordinarily energetic manager of the Pentagon, confident that every problem could be solved. He frequently flew to South Vietnam to get a firsthand impression of the war. As the conflict expanded, however, stalemated at higher and higher levels of violence, McNamara developed doubts about the wisdom of American policies in Vietnam. He became caught between his need to defend the administration's policies and his private skepticism over the outcome of the war and his opposition to the military's efforts to expand it. After McNamara left office to become president of the World Bank, he retreated into silence, refusing to comment on his role in the war.

But McNamara could not escape the ghosts of the Vietnam War. Finally, in 1995, he published the memoir that he had "planned never to write," admitting that he and other members of the Kennedy and Johnson administrations had been "wrong, terribly wrong" and also accepting, at long last, the obligation to explain the mistakes they had made. *In Retrospect* does so at great length, mixing McNamara's recollections with a thorough review of the documentary evidence. Four years later, McNamara revealed the intensity of his search for answers in *Argument Without End,* an attempt to identify ways in which the Vietnam War might have been prevented or ended before it ran its course.[6]

McNamara—a policymaker, not a historian—studies the past in order to draw lessons from it for the present and future. As he notes in *In Retrospect,* he sees the Vietnam War as "a place to start from."[7] Thus his essay here is part of an effort, going back many years, to learn from the mistakes of the Vietnam War and to fulfill his obligations to a younger generation of Americans. At the age of eighty-three, still hurrying through the twilight of his life, he seeks to find a way, through a distillation of his own experience, to ensure that the twenty-first century will be less violent than the twentieth.

Well aware that the end of the Cold War has not brought an end to conflict among nations, McNamara urges his readers to prepare for the new century by abandoning their faith in the old system of power politics. He seeks to transcend the nation-state, to strengthen the United Nations and its system of collective security and to rely more heavily on the rule of law and common moral values to contain conflicts within and between nations. Drawing lessons from the Vietnam War, he wants the United States to avoid unilateral actions abroad. Acutely aware of the imperfectibility of humankind and its institutions, he warns of the continuing danger of the nuclear threat and outlines measures that would eventually bring about a non-nuclear world. His new prescriptions display a profound awareness of past errors of judgment and of the fragility of world peace.

The five lectures on which these essays are based were delivered at the Johns Hopkins University on May 1, 1998. The contributors are grateful to Louis Galambos for suggesting that we address this challenging and difficult topic, and to A. J. R. Russell-Wood, chair of the Department of History, for presiding over these Albert Shaw Memorial Lectures with such skill and grace. At Johns Hopkins, Sarah Springer looked after all the details of our stay, while at Brown Cherrie Guerzon prepared the manuscript for publication.

May the legacy of this volume be a fuller understanding of how the Vietnam War transformed the two nations that fought it.

After Vietnam

The Vietnam War and the Transformation of America

■

CHARLES E. NEU

In the early 1960s, as a graduate student at Harvard University, I began to follow the Vietnam War. It seemed a distant struggle in an exotic land; I never imagined that it would become a major conflict that would bring a sea change in the life of the nation. After I completed my Ph.D. in the history of American foreign relations, I moved to Rice University in Houston, Texas, where the war soon became a major issue for me and many of my students. While I was too old for the draft, those I taught were not so fortunate, and they were bitterly divided over the rights and wrongs of the conflict.

From the start, I was skeptical about American involvement in Vietnam, but I knew I did not understand many aspects of it. After moving to Brown University in 1970, I waited for the literature on the war to develop. Finally, in 1980, I began to teach a seminar on what I called "the American experience in Vietnam." Nine years later I started teaching a lecture course on the war, one that has always been among the most popular courses at the university.

Teaching the war to a younger generation of students was a constant challenge, as was keeping up with the widening stream of scholarship and the far-reaching revisions this new knowledge brought in our understanding of the conflict. My desire to understand, and to write about, the Vietnam War was strengthened by three trips to Vietnam in the 1990s. As I traveled throughout this extraordinarily beautiful country, talking with young people, veterans of the ARVN (Army of the Republic of South Vietnam), and North Vietnamese leaders, I realized that it was a strange and disturbing place to have fought a war, a land that challenged many of our national beliefs and aspirations. My belated trips to Vietnam reminded me that I was part of a generation marked by the war, one that embarked in the 1960s on a long and sad journey to Vietnam that is still far from over.

■

The legacy of the Vietnam War is an unending topic.[1] More than twenty-three years after the fall of Saigon, Vietnam remains an "unfinished war," a conflict that has not found a settled place in the history of the United States. As Arnold R. Isaacs writes, the Vietnam War "lingers in the national memory, hovering over our politics, our culture, and our long, unfinished debate over who we are and what we believe."[2]

Evidence of the turmoil and controversy surrounding the war is virtually everywhere. Many veterans are still trying to make sense of the war and to assess the meaning of their sacrifice. Some have returned to Vietnam, visiting sites where they fought and meeting former enemies, in an effort to put the war behind them.[3] Aging policymakers continue to argue over the conduct of the war and its lessons for American foreign policy.[4] Memories of the Vietnam War had a powerful effect on the way in which President George Bush and his advisers approached the crisis in the Persian Gulf in 1990 and 1991, while the legacy of the war was woven through the 1992 presidential campaign, when the last president of the World War II generation was challenged and defeated by the first president of the Vietnam generation. Four years later, the contrast between President Bill Clinton and his Republican opponent, Robert Dole, again reminded Americans of the immense gap between those who served in World War II and those who avoided serving in Vietnam.[5]

Long after the collapse of South Vietnam, controversy swirls around the major architects of the war, especially former Secretary of Defense Robert S. McNamara. For years he steadfastly refused to explain to the American people what had gone wrong; finally, in April 1995, twenty-seven years after he left office, he published his memoir, *In Retrospect: The Tragedy and Lessons of Vietnam*, admitting that he had made many mistakes and miscalculations. Some commentators praised McNamara for his courage in finally speaking out; others denounced him for an explanation that came, in their judgment, years too late. In a scathing editorial, the *New York Times* claimed that "his regret cannot be huge enough to balance the books for our dead soldiers. The ghosts of those unlived lives circle close around Mr. McNamara. Surely he must in every quiet and prosperous moment hear the ceaseless whispers of those poor boys in the infantry, dying in the tall grass, platoon by platoon, for no purpose. What he took from them cannot be repaid by prime-time apology and stale tears, three decades old." McNamara's confession of error struck a raw nerve, revealing all of the anger still felt by many members of the Vietnam generation.[6]

The unfinished nature of the Vietnam War is also visible in the broader domain of mass culture. The stream of books by soldiers and policymakers seems endless, as does the production of movies and television specials dealing with the war. The popular 1994 movie *Forrest Gump* was, in part, anchored in the Vietnam War; in 1998 Home Box Office transformed Neil Sheehan's *A Bright Shining Lie: John Paul Vann and America in Vietnam* into a television special.[7] And the remarkable staying power of the MIA-POW issue, expressed in both movies and national politics, reveals that, contrary to all logic and evidence, many Americans still believe that the Vietnamese government holds American prisoners.[8] "The pain of the Vietnam War," James Reston Jr. observes, "did not end with the conclusion of hostilities. It continues today. Wounds remain open, waiting to become scars."[9]

I

On the policy level, the American failure in Vietnam brought important changes in the conduct of the nation's diplomacy, weakening all of those Cold War assumptions that had crystallized in the late 1940s and guided American leaders through the late 1960s. The controversy over the war contributed to a softening of the policy of containment and accelerated a reaction against two decades of crisis diplomacy and intervention. Weary of the costs and burdens of the Cold War, Americans became skeptical about the use of force as an instrument of foreign policy and acquired a new sense of the limits of American power abroad.[10] In 1981, when Ronald Reagan came into office, he intensified the Cold War and denounced the Soviet Union as an "evil empire" whose leaders were prepared "to commit any crime, to lie, to cheat" to achieve a communist-dominated world. But Reagan was well aware of the anger and frustration bred by the war and realized that the heavy casualties in Vietnam had brought down Lyndon B. Johnson's presidency. Reagan's extravagant, anti-Soviet rhetoric obscured the fact that he was not about to ask for any painful sacrifices from the American people to achieve his foreign policy goals.[11]

The Vietnam War also divided and hastened the decline of the old foreign policy establishment, a group of centrists and pragmatists that had coalesced during the early Cold War years and had served presidents throughout the postwar decades.[12] Led by former Secretary of State Dean Acheson, this establishment—the "Wise Men," as they were later called—had initially supported Johnson's escalation of the conflict. As the war lengthened, with no end in sight, doubts emerged within this group. But it took the Tet Offensive of January 30, 1968, to shatter their confidence. When Johnson convened his "Wise Men" in March 1968, he discovered that most were disillusioned with the war. Summing up the majority view, Acheson declared: "We can no longer do the job we set out to do in the time we have left, and we must take steps to disengage."[13]

Despite this reversal, the Vietnam War discredited the foreign policy establishment and subjected some of its members to public controversy and humiliation. By the end of the war, the nation's foreign policy was deprived of an anchor that had helped political leaders maintain consensus and continuity.

As the futility of the American effort in South Vietnam became apparent, Congress moved from almost instinctive support of the president's foreign policy before 1965 to aggressive skepticism by 1969. Senator J. William Fulbright, chairman of the Senate Foreign Relations Committee, deplored the "unhinging of traditional constitutional relationships." "The problem," he declared in 1966, "is to find a way to restore the constitutional balance, to find ways by which the Senate can discharge its duties of advice and consent in an era of permanent crisis."[14] Especially in the 1970s, Congress challenged the imperial presidency in a variety of ways. It hired thousands of experts on a whole range of national security issues and attempted to impose restraints on the president, ranging from the War Powers Resolution of 1973 to the prohibition in that same year of all American military activities in Indochina. Eventually it questioned presidential dominance of American foreign policy more vigorously than it had since the middle of the 1930s, and it demanded some degree of partnership in decisions about war and peace. The White House discovered that Congress was now a force to be reckoned with in foreign as well as in domestic affairs.[15]

As the mood on Capitol Hill changed, the Central Intelligence Agency was caught up in Congress's growing suspicion of the presidency and of the national security bureaucracy. In January 1975 the House and Senate voted to create special investigative committees, headed by Representative Otis Pike and Senator Frank Church respectively. These committees gained access to a wide range of CIA files, providing Congress and the American people with their first sustained view of years of CIA operations.[16] Some of the walls of secrecy came tumbling down, with far-reaching consequences. On the practical level, these investigations resulted in new congressional oversight committees before which the agency had to justify both its budget and its proposed covert operations. On the abstract level, they weakened the official American history of the Cold War, which had emphasized American rectitude versus communist expediency and immorality. The inquiries of the Pike and Church committees exposed the darker side of American governmental behavior, bringing the melancholy discovery that American policies had sometimes been callous and careless.[17]

The Vietnam War, therefore, had important consequences even in the short term. In the United States, it altered the assumptions behind the nation's foreign policy, exposed the excesses of the institutions that made it, and brought home the costs of the Cold War to both the American people and the government. In Southeast Asia, the collapse of the Saigon regime in the spring of 1975 brought the unification of Vietnam under communist rule, along with the triumph of communism in Laos and Cambodia.

But the worst fears of American leaders proved groundless. In April 1954 President Dwight D. Eisenhower, in his classic expression of the domino theory, had spoken of the possible sequence of events in Southeast Asia—"the loss of Indochina, of Burma, of Thailand, of the Peninsula, and Indonesia following . . . now you are talking really about millions and millions and millions of people."[18] In the end, however, Eisenhower and other supporters of the domino theory were wrong; the loss of South Vietnam did not undermine America's position in East or Southeast Asia.

II

The Vietnam War was waged, General Phillip B. Davidson observes, not only on a distant battlefield, but also "in the uncharted depths of the American psyche and in the obscurity of our nation's soul."[19] As the conflict wound down and eventually ended, it became apparent that it had changed the mental landscape of the nation. The Vietnam War marked a great divide, separating those who came of age in the triumphant atmosphere following World War II from those who, as Isaacs writes, "grew up into the frustrations and divisions and moral confusion of Vietnam."[20]

The escalation of the Vietnam War in 1965 came only twenty years after the end of World War II, a culminating event in the nation's history.[21] The protagonist in Philip Roth's *American Pastoral* proclaims that after World War II, an "upsurge of energy" swept across the country. "Around us," he continues, "nothing was lifeless. Sacrifice and constraint were over. The Depression had disappeared. Everything was in motion. The lid was off. Americans were to start over again, en masse, everyone in it together. . . . The miraculous conclusion of this towering event, the clock of history reset and a whole people's aims limited no longer by the past."[22] At home the end of the war ushered in a period of unprecedented prosperity and optimism, which historian James T. Patterson characterizes as a time of "grand expectations." Abroad the nation moved to the center of the international system, entering a web of global entanglements in a new era of American predominance.[23]

The defeat of the Axis powers gave new life to old national myths, confirming a whole cluster of beliefs about America's destiny, innocence, and invincibility that were deeply rooted in the nation's past.[24] Early in their history, Americans developed distinctive visions of their nation and its future. America could be imagined as a redeemer nation or, in John Winthrop's phrase, as a "City upon a Hill," chosen by God to set an example for an unregenerate world. Or America could be conceived as a republican experiment, undertaken in defiance of history and uncertain in its outcome.[25] Or it could be seen as an expanding frontier where, in a series of conflicts stretching over several centuries, the American spirit was renewed. At the core of this myth of "regeneration through violence," Richard Slotkin writes, was the savage war, one in which Americans "must cross the border into 'Indian country' and experience a 'regression' to a more primitive and natural condition of life so that the false values of the 'metropolis' can be purged and a new, purified social contract enacted."[26]

In the early years of the republic, America seemed an experiment, for the Founding Fathers knew that they had launched the nation on a bold and difficult journey. Threatened by European monarchies and uncertain of the safety of their republican form of government, the revolutionary generation was wary of foreign entanglements. The United States, to be sure, was a promised land, but one that should lead the world through the power of its example.[27] In his Fourth of July speech in 1821, John Quincy Adams said, "America goes not abroad in search of monsters to destroy. She is the well-wisher to the freedom and independence of all. She is the champion only of her own."[28]

In the nineteenth century, as the nation expanded across the continent, survived the ordeal of the Civil War, and grew more confident in its power and the durability of its institutions, the ideas of America as an experiment or a promised land gave way to the idea of America as a nation with a sacred mission, unique in its virtue and destiny. Toward the end of the century, more and more Americans concluded that the United States should spread the blessings of liberty and plenty to other lands.[29] In 1885 the Reverend Josiah Strong, in his best-seller *Our Country,* proclaimed that Americans were a

> race of unequaled energy, with all the majesty of numbers and the might of wealth behind it—the representative, let us hope, of the largest liberty, the purest Christianity, the highest civilization—having developed peculiarly aggressive traits calculated to impress its institutions upon mankind, will spread itself over the earth. . . . Is there room for reasonable doubt that this race . . . is destined to dispossess many weaker races, assimilate others, and mold the remainder, until, in a very true and important sense, it has Anglo-Saxonized mankind?[30]

Over the course of the twentieth century, as the United States was drawn deeper into world politics, this belief in national righteousness and providential destiny grew stronger. Involvement in two world wars and the Cold War transformed America, in Walter A. McDougall's phrase, into a "crusader state," convinced of the superiority of its institutions and way of life and intent on imposing them on the outside world.[31] At the start of the Cold War, President Harry S. Truman expressed his belief that "God has created us and brought us to our present position of power and strength for some great purpose"; near the end of the Cold War, President Ronald Reagan said that he had "always believed that this anointed land was set apart in an uncommon way, that a divine plan placed this great continent here between the oceans to be found by people from every corner of the earth who had a special love of faith and freedom."[32]

Inevitably, America's efforts to fulfill such exalted ideals brought conflicts with other peoples and the emergence of a distinctive war story. From the seventeenth century through the end of the nineteenth century, white Americans fought Indians on what the former regarded as the borders of civilization. This nonwhite enemy sometimes overwhelmed and defeated small groups of U.S. soldiers or settlers, but such defeats in the end served as a prelude to victory. Whether the nation's enemy was Indians or, later, Mexicans, Spaniards, Filipinos, Germans, or Japanese, every foe was defeated by American forces.[33] During World War II the nation's war story, like so many other aspects of its history, reached a climax, especially in the Pacific War against Japan. After the initial surprise attack on the American garrison at Pearl Harbor, the war became a series of bitter, savage campaigns, a "war without mercy" on distant Pacific islands, where Japanese forces were overwhelmed by the superior might of the American war machine.[34]

During the postwar years, the nation's heroic war story encountered new and troubling realities. The Cold War, along with the atomic age, brought a loss of focus, for it was difficult to imagine victory in a large-scale clash with the Soviet Union. With the spread of communism to many parts of the world and the emergence of a domestic Red scare, the nation's enemy became both diffuse and omnipresent. And inevitably setbacks occurred, such as the triumph of communism in China in 1949—a stunning rejection of more than one hundred years of efforts by America to change China.[35]

III

At the time of John F. Kennedy's inauguration, the Cold War, well into its second decade, had brought countless crises and covert interventions and a bloody war in Korea that ended in stalemate. The mood of the new administration, however, was tough and energetic. Kennedy wanted a more active policy of containment, especially in the Third World, and was convinced that the nation could afford ambitious programs both at home and abroad.[36] His inaugural address, devoted almost entirely to Cold War issues, was a stirring call to action and sacrifice, a plea for heroic engagement in "a long twilight struggle" against communism. "Let every nation know," the young president proclaimed, "whether it wishes us well or ill, that we shall pay any price, bear any burden, meet any hardship, support any friend, oppose any foe to assure the survival and the success of liberty. . . . Since this country was founded, each generation of Americans has been summoned to give testimony to its national loyalty. The graves of young Americans who answered the call to service surround the globe."[37]

Kennedy acted on this rhetoric, launching ambitious programs such as the Peace Corps, Food for Peace, the Alliance for Progress, and landing a man on the moon; confronting the Soviet Union in a series of crises; and increasing America's commitment to South Vietnam. In pursuing these initiatives abroad, Kennedy carried the American people with him. They were willing to support his administration in the "long twilight struggle" that had no end in sight.[38] The war in Vietnam was a part of that struggle, a war where it seemed Americans could test their character and work out their special destiny.[39] In the early 1960s the scale of the war remained small, allowing room for individuals to make their mark. One American general, in a talk to advisers attached to the South Vietnamese Army, summed up the prevailing attitude when he remarked, "It isn't much of a war, but it's the only war we've got, so enjoy it."[40]

On the policy level, Kennedy and his advisers were divided and often confused about the war.[41] On the mythic level, however, the war had a deep appeal. As John Hellmann writes, "Vietnam promised . . . the qualities of America's remembered frontier triumphs: remoteness from dangerous confrontations with a major European power, a savage enemy who could be righteously hunted down, a wilderness landscape in which the American could renew his virtues where the European had proved only his vices, and the Asian people America historically saw as the appointed beneficiaries of its destiny." The attraction of the Vietnam War, conceived in these terms, was revealed in the extraordinary success of Robin Moore's *The Green Berets,* published in 1965. In Moore's adventure tale, a few dedicated individuals pursued America's mission in the Vietnamese wilderness. Kennedy's emphasis on the Green Berets and counterinsurgency warfare had a powerful resonance in the American past.[42]

Kennedy's call for sacrifice and heroic engagement abroad affected many young people. Philip Caputo, who landed at Danang, South Vietnam, in March 1965, with the first American ground combat troops, remembers how "for Americans who did not come of age in the early sixties, it may be hard to grasp what those years were like—the pride and overpowering self-assurance that prevailed. Most of the thirty-five hundred men in our brigade, born during or immediately after World War II, were shaped by that era, the age of Kennedy's Camelot. We went overseas full of illusions, for which the intoxicating atmosphere of those years was as much to blame as our youth."[43]

Illusions of this sort, however, did not prepare Americans for the reality of the Vietnam War. Leaders of the U.S. government, preoccupied with the Cold War and confident of American power and technology, viewed the war in Vietnam in abstract terms, as a test of the nation's will and determination to combat communist expansion in the Third World. They found it hard to focus on Vietnam itself, on either its history and culture or the nature of the revolution there. On his first trip to South Vietnam, in May 1962, Secretary of Defense McNamara revealed this cursory approach. After spending only forty-eight hours talking to officials and traveling in the field, he told reporters that he had seen "a great deal of South Vietnam" and "acquired a 'good feel'" for conditions in the country.[44]

Most of the nation's high-ranking military commanders, still basking in the glow of their great triumph in World War II, had a can-do attitude and pushed for escalation. In July 1965, when Johnson and his advisers were debating the escalation of the war, the president asked General Earle G. Wheeler, chairman of the Joint Chiefs of Staff, what leaders in Hanoi would do if the United States increased its forces. Wheeler admitted that the North Vietnamese might respond, but he insisted that they could not put more than 25 percent of their 250,000-man army into South Vietnam. Wheeler was confident that if they did so, the United States would "cream them."[45] In hindsight, it is clear that the president's senior military commanders suffered from what Neil Sheehan terms the "disease of victory" and that they approached the struggle in South Vietnam with a certain arrogance and complacency. While their estimates of the magnitude of the challenge varied, they found it hard to imagine how America could not prevail in such a small and seemingly primitive country.[46]

Young Americans who went to fight in South Vietnam had

grown up greatly influenced by World War II. Their image of war was shaped by the memories of their fathers and by the movies, especially movies with John Wayne. By the early 1960s, Wayne was a major cultural icon, a folk hero who had come to represent the old West and the American soldier. As Garry Wills writes, all Americans "are entangled in his story, by the dreams he shaped or inhibited . . . by the things he validated and those he scorned, by the particular definition he gave to 'being American.' . . . Down the street of the twentieth-century imagination, that figure is still walking toward us—graceful, menacing, inescapable."[47] Ron Kovic, who was born in 1946, remembers *Sands of Iwo Jima* (1949), in which Sergeant Stryker, played by Wayne, led his squad of Marines in a charge up Mount Suribachi, only to be killed just before reaching the top. Wayne and the Marines were his heroes. The Marine recruiters who visited his high school looked just as they had appeared in the movies and "spoke in a very beautiful way about the exciting history of the marines and how they had never lost and how America had never been defeated." Kovic loved the Marine Corps hymn.[48]

Americans who stayed at home, lifted up by the tidal wave of postwar prosperity and inspired by Kennedy's vision of a "New Frontier," could not imagine the way in which the war and the turmoil of the 1960s would affect their lives. "The death-littered valleys of Vietnam . . . changed the way I thought of my family, my nation, my faith, and myself," writes James Carroll. Carroll had grown up with a "vivid and continuous sense of connection with America." As a two-year-old, he had been at Franklin D. Roosevelt's last inauguration, and in the postwar years, as he attended one inauguration after another, he realized that they were "like a sacrament of the streets to me, rituals of rebirth, the one true American gala, a quadrennial instance of Jefferson's 'peaceful revolution.'" The Vietnam War transformed Carroll and his sense of America until, at Richard M. Nixon's second inauguration, in January 1973, he shook his fist and "cursed the president of the United States"—an act that measured the distance he had come from his "youthful worship of these men."[49]

IV

In 1965, as the war in Vietnam grew rapidly in scale and intensity, it became apparent that President Johnson would have trouble explaining this conflict to the American people, linking it to the nation's sense of mission or to its traditional war story. In mid-1965 the government produced a film entitled *Why Viet-Nam,* which opened with Johnson reading a letter from a Midwestern woman asking why her son was in Vietnam. The president responded by asking a question of his own: "Why must young Americans born into a land exultant with hope and with golden promise, toil and suffer and sometimes die in such a remote and distant place? The answer," the president concluded, "like the war itself, is not an easy one." As the film progresses, the narrator attempts to answer Johnson's question, justifying the war as an effort to honor America's commitment to the government of South Vietnam and to prevent communism from spreading into Southeast Asia.[50] But officials in Washington could not construct a convincing narrative for the war; as it continued, they had more and more difficulty explaining, in Tom Engelhardt's words, "the story of a slow-motion defeat inflicted by a nonwhite people in a frontier war in which the statistics of American victory seemed everywhere evident."[51]

As the war lengthened and casualties mounted, no aspect of the struggle confirmed the traditional American war story. Enemy forces were largely invisible, blending in with the peasantry, hiding in remote jungle or mountain sanctuaries, and generally able to control the pace of the conflict, striking American units when it was advantageous to do so. Main force Viet Cong (VC) and North Vietnamese Army (NVA) soldiers were formidable opponents, displaying a fanatical devotion to their cause and great ingenuity and persistence in exploiting the land and people, whether in building elaborate tunnel complexes underground or keeping supplies flowing down the Ho Chi Minh Trail. By American standards, VC and NVA units took staggering casualties, but time after time they were able to withdraw and rebuild their strength.[52] Worse still, enemy soldiers acquired an almost heroic stature. "In our minds," William Broyles Jr. remembers, "the enemy wasn't another soldier, a man like us. He was mysterious and elusive—a vision from the unknown, a bogeyman with terrible powers rising up out of the earth. . . . The primitive methods that the enemy adopted in the face of our technology made him that much more formidable."[53] And the government in Hanoi portrayed President Ho Chi Minh, its legendary leader, as a benevolent grandfather who sought only the freedom and independence of his people.[54]

The big-unit war of 1965 and later, with its search-and-destroy missions and massive use of artillery and airpower, was far removed from the earlier version of the war embodied in Kennedy's counterinsurgency strategy and in the myth of the Green Berets. As Johnson transformed the conflict, he lost sight of how, as John Hellmann writes, this new war "would look to an American youth uncomfortable with the affluence, bureaucracy, technology, and racism of their society."[55] Leading intellectuals of the antiwar movement, such as the novelists Norman Mailer, Mary McCarthy, and Susan Sontag, exploited these anxieties, idealizing North Vietnam as a harmonious, pastoral society while depicting America as a decadent, violent, machinelike empire. The antiwar movement began to gain the high ground in its struggle with the American government over the meaning of the war.[56]

While the enemy in Vietnam was mysterious and, to some Americans, heroic, America's allies in Saigon seemed venal and corrupt, more interested in graft than in combat and unable to rally their people behind a common cause or to create an effective military force. The client state that America supported in South Vietnam for more than twenty years stumbled along, led (after the assassination of President Ngo Dinh Diem in November 1963) by military officers with little understanding of American politics or culture and with little ability to appeal to the American people.[57]

American officials who dealt with South Vietnamese leaders were puzzled and frustrated. Assistant Secretary of State William P. Bundy characterized President Nguyen Van Thieu and Vice President Nguyen Cao Ky, who came to power in 1967, as "the bottom of the barrel, absolutely the bottom of the barrel," while Secretary of State Dean Rusk asked the American ambassador in Saigon, "Is there any way we can shake the main body of the Vietnamese leadership by the scruff of the neck?"[58] American troops who worked with their South Vietnamese counterparts were initially shocked, then angered, by the unwillingness of many ARVN (Army of the Republic of Vietnam) units to fight aggressively. Occasionally American officers were impressed by the dedication and skill of South Vietnamese commanders, but more often relations between American and South Vietnamese troops were tense. Robert Mason, an American helicopter pilot, had heard stories from other pilots about problems carrying ARVN troops. Even so, he was unprepared for the ARVN Rangers who, when he carried them into a landing zone, refused to get off until his crew chief threatened them with a pistol. "Whose war was this, anyway?" he wondered.[59]

In the summer and fall of 1965, as American troops and materiel poured into South Vietnam, the expectations of the U.S. officers and their men were high. Sometimes they received unpleasant surprises. In August of that year, Marine units assaulted a VC regiment in the central coastal area of South Vietnam. On the second day of the battle the VC, badly hurt, slipped away, but the Americans were amazed at the stamina of their new enemy. As one Marine general, a veteran of Saipan and Iwo Jima, put it: "I thought that once they ran up against our first team they wouldn't stand and fight. I made a miscalculation." Still, most American commanders believed that their forces would inflict unacceptable casualties on enemy troops and break their will to resist.[60]

Both generals and soldiers soon realized that the war in Vietnam did not fit their preconceived notions. By the autumn of 1965, Philip Caputo remembers, "what had begun [in March] as an adventurous expedition had turned into an exhausting, indecisive war of attrition in which we fought for no other cause than our own survival."[61] The enemy was elusive, the climate and terrain treacherous, and peasants in the countryside often unfriendly. The pattern of warfare that emerged was formless yet lethal, consisting of haphazard, episodic contacts with the enemy and few set-piece battles. In contrast to World War II and Korea, Vietnam was a war without a front, without any clear direction or momentum, in which progress was measured by the number of enemy troops killed rather than by the amount of territory gained. Combat had a circular quality; American units would often patrol the same territory over and over, engaging in fleeting contacts with the enemy, or take an objective and then abandon it.[62]

For Harold G. Moore, who arrived in South Vietnam in September 1965, doubts began to emerge in early 1966, when he led his brigade in a campaign against NVA troops in a densely populated rice-farming region along the coast of central Vietnam. After heavy fighting, American units prevailed. But soon enemy troops returned to the area, and twice in the spring Moore's brigade returned to drive them out. How, Moore wondered, could the United States ever win, if the South Vietnamese government could not reestablish control in such newly cleared areas?[63]

For combat soldiers, the war bred confusion. Most were ignorant of Vietnam's past and knew little about the history of the French and American wars there. When William Broyles Jr. tried to explain to his radioman why American forces were fighting, he found that his answer, "We're here to help South Vietnam stay independent," was too abstract. His next response, "Our mission is to protect the Da Nang vital area," brought the question "Why is Da Nang a vital area?" "I guess," Broyles explained, "it's because of all the American support troops back there." "Yeah," said the radioman, "but why are they there?" Completing the circle, Broyles answered, "Well, to support us."[64]

As the war went on, the confusion deepened and old myths dissolved. Soldiers arrived in Vietnam with images of war derived from John Wayne movies; as they gained experience, however, his name was used to identify individual acts that looked good in the movies but that would bring death in combat. As Samuel Hynes observes, "It is a sign of how completely the old values had faded that Wayne, hero of the Westerns and war movies that the Vietnam War generation had grown up on, and the embodiment of what seemed a particularly American kind of independent courage, had become a soldier's joke, an anti-hero, everybody's example of how *not* to fight a war."[65] For some American officers and soldiers, the war retained a clarity and sense of moral purpose; for others it brought disillusionment and a loss of faith. Tobias Wolff, who served as adviser to an ARVN battalion in the Mekong Delta, noticed that a nearby American unit seemed to be in a state of despair. "At Dong Tam," he writes, "I saw something that wasn't allowed for in the national myth—our capacity for collective despair. . . . The resolute imperial will was all played out here at the empire's fringe, lost in rancor and mud. Here were pharaoh's chariots engulfed; his horsemen confused; and all his magnificence dismayed."[66]

In Vietnam a troubling reversal occurred in the image of American soldiers. In World War II they had generally been hailed as liberators, often aided by resistance groups and surrounded by cheering crowds as they occupied towns and cities. In Vietnam, American units that moved through the countryside encountered a wary peasantry, especially in areas controlled by the VC. Many villages were emptied of young men and surrounded by deadly booby traps and land mines. Confronted with an often hostile population and what seemed at first glance a primitive, repugnant way of life, many Americans units retaliated against villagers.[67] David Donovan, an officer who had received training in Vietnamese history, culture, and language, was appalled by the "contempt and disrespect" most American soldiers showed toward the Vietnamese and by "the generally abysmal relations between Americans and the Vietnamese villagers." And General Creighton W. Abrams, who became General William C. Westmoreland's deputy commander in May 1967 and replaced him in June 1968, remembered that "Americans as a whole had trouble with the whole idea of the Vietnamese. Their color was a little different, their eyes were a little different, they were kind of small—those kinds of differences tend to bother Americans."[68]

Soon the war began to produce disturbing visual images. In August 1965 Morley Safer and a CBS news crew accompanied a Marine patrol as it moved into the village of Cam Ne. Both Safer and, later, the American public were shocked to see U.S. soldiers casually setting fire to the huts in the village while Vietnamese peasants cowered in fear or begged for their homes to be spared. Americans were accustomed to viewing their soldiers as liberators, not avengers.[69] American units with good leadership understood the importance of treating villagers decently and trying to win the peasantry over to their side. But occasionally discipline broke down. The worst incident occurred in the village of My Lai in March 1968, when more than 400 civilians, including women and children, were killed by American troops. Not until December 1969, when poignant photographs by a military cameraman appeared across ten pages of *Life* magazine, did the American people realize the extent of the atrocity, and the extent to which the Vietnam War had transformed the behavior of at least some American soldiers.[70]

V

Most Americans found it difficult to judge the wisdom and progress of the war. Information from South Vietnam could be read in different ways, and assessments by the nation's leaders varied widely. In November 1967 Senator Robert F. Kennedy, rejecting the administration's geopolitical arguments, said on *Face the Nation,* "We're killing South Vietnamese, we're killing children, we're killing women, we're killing innocent people . . . because we don't want to have the war fought on American soil . . . because [the communists are] 12,000 miles away and they might get to be 11,000 miles away." That same month, however, Westmoreland, convinced that the crossover point had been reached (when the losses suffered by enemy units exceeded their ability to replace them), told the National Press Club in Washington, "We have reached an important point when the end begins to come into view." In two years or less, Westmoreland predicted, it would be possible to reduce American ground forces and turn more of the fighting over to the South Vietnamese.[71] It took the Tet Offensive of January 30, 1968, to convince most Americans that Westmoreland was wrong. The war had become a killing field for Americans and Vietnamese with no end in sight.

Throughout the remainder of 1968, fighting was intense and peace negotiations deadlocked. When Nixon came into office, his policy of "peace with honor"—with its gradual withdrawal of American troops, transfer of responsibility for the war to the South Vietnamese, and search for a negotiated settlement—seemed plausible to many Americans.[72] The signing of the Paris Peace Accords in January 1973 confirmed their hopes that somehow the nation's objectives could be achieved. But the dramatic collapse of South Vietnam in the spring of 1975, ending with the fall of Saigon on April 30, destroyed any illusions that remained. The final scenes of panic and desperation shocked the nation. Americans were not prepared for this sort of flight.[73]

The outcome of the Vietnam War seemed almost beyond understanding. How had the war become a quagmire? How had the nation become so sharply divided? How had the architects of the war miscalculated so badly? In short, where had John Wayne's America gone wrong?

Some Americans concluded that the Vietnam War revealed deep

flaws in American society and foreign policy. They urged the nation to engage in a fundamental rethinking of Cold War assumptions and to accept a reduced role in world politics.[74] In 1977 George F. Kennan, the author of the policy of containment, asked his countrymen to consider "whether the great miscalculations which led us into the folly of Vietnam were not something more than just the shortsightedness of a few individuals—whether they did not in fact reflect a certain unfitness of the system as a whole for the conceiving and executing of ambitious political-military ventures far from our own shores."[75]

Other public figures disagreed, arguing that the war was lost at home, not in Southeast Asia, and that the final collapse of the Saigon government came only because the United States reduced aid to South Vietnam and allowed the North Vietnamese Army to carry out a conventional military offensive. Convinced that the subsequent harshness of North Vietnam's rule vindicated the "moral soundness" of America's intervention, they were angry over the outcome. In the end, America appeared weak and helpless, irresolute and lacking in courage.[76] Supporters of the American war effort were determined to rebuild the confidence, moral resolve, and military strength of the nation, so that America could resume its rightful primacy in world affairs. "For too long," Ronald Reagan declared in August 1980, "we have lived with the Vietnam Syndrome. This is a lesson for all of us in Vietnam. If we are forced to fight, we must have the means and the determination to prevail, or we will not have what it takes to secure peace. And while we are at it, let us tell those who fought in that war, that we will never again ask young men to fight and possibly die in a war our government is afraid to let them win."[77]

Those who served in Vietnam, whether in high-level policy positions or in ground combat, were frustrated by the way in which the war ended. General Westmoreland blamed his political superiors for the defeat. "Had the president allowed a change in strategy and taken advantage of the enemy's weaknesses," he maintains, "the

North Vietnamese doubtless would have broken."[78] William E. Colby, who directed important CIA programs in Vietnam, believed that a counterinsurgency strategy would have won the war. Over the final evacuation efforts from Saigon, he remembers, "hung the tragedy of this waste of lives and the years of effort of both Vietnamese and Americans who had hoped that Vietnam might develop in freedom."[79]

Severely wounded soldiers were especially disillusioned. Ron Kovic's terrible wound—which left the lower half of his body paralyzed—led to a loss of faith in the nation and its leaders. Bitterly he wrote, "I have given my dead swinging dick for America. I have given my numb young dick for democracy. . . . Yes, I gave my dead dick for John Wayne." Lewis Puller, also seriously wounded, had been apolitical before leaving for Vietnam in the summer of 1968, accepting the judgment of leaders in Washington. Returning to America, he concluded that the war was a mistake and "began to feel that my own sacrifice and that of all of us who had fought the war were meaningless."[80] Many other veterans who had fought in what had become a lost cause were also unable to find meaning in their sacrifices, or to understand what had gone wrong to deprive the nation of victory.[81]

Americans had entered the Vietnam War with the expectation that a distinctively American story would unfold. When the conflict developed in unexpected ways, as John Hellmann observes, "the true nature of the larger story of America itself became the subject of intense cultural dispute. On the deepest level, the legacy of Vietnam is the disruption of our story, of our explanation of the past and vision of the future."[82] The collapse of South Vietnam left many Americans with a sense of loss and betrayal, as if, in the words of Arnold Isaacs, "it was some vital piece of America's vision of itself—trust, self-confidence, social order, belief in the benevolence and ordained success of American power—which had disappeared in the mountain mists and vine-tangled jungles of Vietnam, and which so many Americans wanted so desperately to get back."[83]

The war had seared the consciousness of an entire generation and altered the mood of the nation.

Most Americans sensed that the nation had entered a new era after Vietnam, one that was filled with divisions, uncertainties, and moral confusions, both at home and abroad. After 1974, James T. Patterson writes, "the United States, so powerful for much of the postwar period, seemed adrift, unable to reconcile the races (or the classes or the sexes) at home or to perform as effectively on the world stage."[84] Neither the powerful rhetoric of President Reagan in the 1980s, nor the stunning success of the Persian Gulf War in 1991, nor the collapse of the Soviet Union and the end of the Cold War in 1991 could restore the old sense of innocence, destiny, and national self-confidence.

Amid all the currents and countercurrents of contemporary American life, a yearning for a more cohesive, heroic past mingled with anxieties about the future. The nation's nostalgia was revealed in 1998 in the remarkable critical and box-office success of Steven Spielberg's World War II film *Saving Private Ryan.* While it contained horrifying scenes of warfare, in the end *Saving Private Ryan* took Americans back to the nation's moment of glory, when its leaders were decent and wise and its cause just.[85] And in *An Empire Wilderness,* journalist Robert D. Kaplan documented Americans' unease about the future, about the erosion of national unity. His book is an unsettling vision of America in the twenty-first century, a nation in which old loyalties and allegiances are dissolving into an emerging transnational society. The nation that sent young men off to war in distant Vietnam in the mid-1960s is gone. What, if anything, Kaplan wonders, would citizens of this new, globalized America be willing to fight and die for?[86]

From Metaphor to Quagmire

The Domestic Legacy of the Vietnam War

■

BRIAN BALOGH

Two moments sum up the indirect and convoluted nature of my relationship to Vietnam. The first took place at Phillips Academy in Andover, Massachusetts, in the spring of 1970. As college campuses around the nation exploded in reaction to the "incursion" into Cambodia, we staged our own protest at this elite prep school. Inspired by the student activism that older siblings reported from Ivy League campuses, we challenged the establishment ourselves: we ripped off the ties that were required attire at the time. Then, on the steps of the administration building, we burned them! This experience opened my eyes to politics at the same time that it connected me to a web of friendships with other students who shared an emerging worldview. That vision consisted of much more than war-stimulated protest, but protest was the price of admission. Unlike the civil rights protesters who had earlier risked public censure, their jobs, and in some cases their lives for a cause, we risked very little in burning our ties or, later, in college, chanting "Off the pigs."

The second moment occurred fifteen years later in the library of the Johns Hopkins University. I had come to my dissertation topic—on the challenge to the authority of experts in the 1970s—in part through studying an extensive literature that cited Vietnam (and Watergate) as the reason. Like many fourth-year graduate students, I despaired of ever saying anything new on my subject. After a bit of archival research, it occurred to me that the reasons for this challenge to authority lay deeper in the social structure and in the way that expertise had been produced and nurtured in the post–World War II state. I ended up writing a dissertation and book that argued against the prevailing literature, the sine qua non of a successful academic career. Once again, my indirect contact with a war that caused so much damage to so many individuals and the nation as a whole had redounded to my benefit.

For millions of Americans, Vietnam had direct and tragic consequences. As others lost friends to the war, I made them. It is even likely that I was spared direct contact with the horror of Vietnam because I rose from the lower middle to upper middle class on the tide of a war-induced inflationary economy that particularly favored my father's jewelry business. This is not to say that my inverse relationship to the tragedy of the war was unique. Like many others who shared my race (white) and eventual economic status, the crucial variable was the degree of direct contact with Vietnam the place. For those who were there, likely to be there, or had many friends there, tragedy was unavoidable. Those for whom Vietnam was a topic, a cause, and (as I discuss below) eventually a metaphor recognized this tragedy but were less likely to be its direct victim.

■

It's 1991. Walter Sobcek, a gun-toting vet whose favorite expression is "Am I wrong?" has just returned the ashes of his bowling buddy Donny to the Pacific. Like most of Walter's gestures, it doesn't quite work out as planned. The coastal winds sweep up what's left of the surfer-turned-bowler and blow his ashes right into the face of Jeff Lebowski. Walter apologizes, embracing the ash-strewn Lebowski. Lebowski has come a long way. Thirty years ago, he helped write the Port Huron Statement—the embodiment of the New Left's critique of mainstream America. He's Walter's bowling partner now, and he even has a picture in his house of Nixon bowling. Exasperated, Lebowski pushes Walter away. "What the fuck does anything have to do with Vietnam?" he pleads.

This scene is the denouement of the 1998 film *The Big Lebowski.* Besides the slapstick high jinks of Walter and Lebowski, the film offers a deft commentary on what is left of the sixties. For the most part, it's a few expressions that Lebowski lives by—"far out," "man," "fucking a"—and the name he goes by: "the Dude." It's also the tenuous community created around bowling. In other words, not much. The sixties are scattered to the winds, part of the dust of history—like Donny's ashes and the tumbleweed blowing across the scrub at the opening of the film. The one exception is Walter's obsession with the Nam. Even while delivering the homespun eulogy for his buddy Donny—who certainly never set foot in Vietnam—Walter goes into a lengthy commentary on the war. It is this digression that sets off Lebowski.

Lebowski and Walter represent two extremes that have characterized our collective memory of the sixties. Lebowski's forte is forgetting. True, he experiences the occasional acid flashback. But even the flashbacks are updated: they feature Saddam Hussein in a bowling shirt, not LBJ in a gray suit. Walter, on the other hand, conflates everything into Vietnam. Taking his own lecture about the need to "draw a line" seriously, he pulls his revolver and threatens to shoot another bowler over a disputed score.

This essay places the domestic impact of the Vietnam War in historical context. Because Vietnam was such a wrenching emotional experience, because it was so visible—"the television war"—because it affected the lives of so many Americans, because the nation felt besieged by problems in its wake, and, most significantly, because even the most optimistic Americans could find little that was positive about the experience, there has been a tendency to blame much that has gone wrong in America on the Vietnam War. The legacy of Vietnam has proven to be just as unending as the conflict itself seemed. In foreign policy and military affairs, the lingering power of the "Vietnam syndrome" is well known. The effect in domestic affairs, I contend, has been equally strong, but far less well recognized. At home, Vietnam has come to represent the decline of authority, a new level of social and political conflict, and the fragmentation of national identity. This is not to deny the more tangible legacies of Vietnam—the cost in human lives, in dollars, in political ambitions—which are enormous and well documented. The most powerful of these domestic legacies, however, is the metaphor that Vietnam has become for turmoil and decline.

That metaphor, evoking many of the strong emotions that were unleashed by the war, has obscured more than it has enlightened. While Vietnam as metaphor has been good for Hollywood and perhaps even aided the healing process, it has been bad for history. After reviewing the legacies of Vietnam and exploring the metaphor, this essay concludes by sketching some of the structural changes in American society and politics that, in conjunction with the war, are part of a more balanced historical assessment of the turbulent times we so easily associate with Vietnam. Even in a book about the legacy of Vietnam, not everything has to be about Vietnam.

The Legacies of Vietnam

The noun most often associated with Vietnam is *tragedy. Nightmare* and *quagmire* are close seconds. Among the verbs, *mired, bogged down, drawn into, trapped,* and *traumatized* are all leading candidates. No wonder most Americans sought to forget this war even before it ended. They were momentarily successful. "Self-conscious collective amnesia," to use George Herring's phrase, gripped the country in the immediate aftermath of the war. "Today Americans can regain the sense of pride that existed before Vietnam," President Gerald Ford told an audience at Tulane shortly before the fall of Saigon in 1975. "But it cannot be achieved refighting a war that is finished." In their haste to forget the war, Americans forgot also the men and women who fought it. Sensitive to the mood of the nation that they returned to, many veterans aided this attempt to avoid thinking about the war. "We got home and went into the airport," one vet reported. "We went into the bathroom and there was uniforms scattered all over. Guys were just leaving them there. We threw ours away, put on civilian clothes and never mentioned Vietnam again."[1]

Although America tried its hardest to forget Vietnam, it could not. By the 1980s, the amnesia had subsided. Some pundits even predicted that Vietnam would "haunt us forever. It is a war everyone wanted to forget—but can't." Most veterans were not able to leave their experience behind in airport bathrooms. The living memory that they embodied and increasingly articulated punctured the silence that at first surrounded the war. So did the scholarly debate that soon broke out about the reasons for America's military failure. Hollywood had taken the plunge by the late seventies. Eventually, even network television invaded Vietnam. "It's back! Napalm, fire fights, body bags, Hueys, rice paddies, Victor Charlie, search-and-destroy, the quagmire, the living room war," the *New York Times* reported in August 1987. A common phrase used by grunts in Vietnam best sums up the conflicted attitude of Americans about the war in the decade after the fall of Saigon: "Fuck it, it don't mean nothin'." Dismissive in its intent, the phrase paradoxically evoked an act that entails procreative and intimate joining that, for the moment, embodied everything. The offspring produced by this illicit union—its legacies—seemed to grow exponentially during the 1980s.[2]

Today, the list of those legacies is formidable. The most somber and irrevocable one is death and bodily injury. Michael Hunt estimates that 1.4 million civilians and combatants died from 1965 through 1972—the period during which American troops fought. Another 300,000 men, women, and children lost their lives in the subsequent two and a half years. More than 58,000 of those who died in Vietnam were American soldiers. Deaths among South Vietnamese forces numbered 220,000. In comparison with previous wars, the average age of the American soldiers killed was extraordinarily low: 60 percent of those who died were between seventeen and twenty-one. In Vietnam 270,000 Americans were wounded, 21,000 sustaining disabilities. The war also disabled 1.4 million Vietnamese, and it created half a million Vietnamese orphans.[3]

As with all wars, there was massive dislocation. By 1972 a population of 18 million in South Vietnam supported close to 10 million refugees. With the fall of Saigon, 1 million people fled the country, many losing their lives on the open seas. Approximately 2 million Vietnamese refugees have moved to the United States.[4]

Those Americans fortunate enough to have escaped death or injury in Vietnam still faced the disruption of their lives and, for many, the searing memory of combat. In all, more than 2 million Americans went to Vietnam. Those who served were drawn from a pool of more than 26 million men of draft age over the course of America's involvement in the war. The average age of those who served was nineteen years old. As the most visible reminder of the war, veterans were sometimes spit at or demeaned in other ways. More often, they were ignored.[5]

Despite the carnage, some have argued that the most significant legacy of Vietnam was a spiritual one. Vietnam shattered the myth of American invincibility. We lost our sense of omnipotence. Characteristically, former Secretary of Defense Robert McNamara presented the problem in its most understated guise. Summing up the lessons of Vietnam, he noted that "we failed to recognize that in international affairs . . . there may be problems for which there are no immediate solutions." "At times," McNamara cautioned, "we may have to live with an imperfect, untidy world." It followed that humility should replace hubris as the touchstone of American foreign policy. Stanley Hoffman stated the problem more baldly: "At the root of this tree of evils one finds an extraordinary arrogance . . . , a self intoxicating confidence in our capacity to manipulate other societies."[6]

For many, the presumption that American foreign policy was premised on a moral foundation was undermined. Paul Boyer, summing up America's experience in Vietnam, used a theological trope: "America lost its innocence and learned the meaning of sin." Did America lose in Vietnam "its right to appeal to morals?" asked Günter Grass. Whether swayed by charges of genocide or convinced that political leaders had been "derelict" in their duty, some framed the war as a crime, not merely a blunder.[7]

Innocence and omnipotence lost shattered the perception of American exceptionalism. In the wake of the war in Vietnam and the problems it exposed at home, the United States would have its hands full simply with the mundane tasks faced by every nation-state. General Maxwell Taylor summed up the chastened attitude about American exceptionalism in 1978. Noting that Americans had felt that they could "go almost any place and do almost anything" after World War II, Taylor warned that "henceforth we're going to have trouble feeding and keeping happy our own growing population just as every other nation is. This is not a time for our government to get out on limbs which are not essential." Vietnam tested America's will to reshape the world in its own image and the claim of its citizens to be a special people. In the words of George Ball, Vietnam was a "tragic defeat for America. Not in the military terms of the battlefield, but a defeat for our political authority and moral influence abroad and for our sense of mission and cohesion at home."[8]

The one lesson in foreign policy that everybody seemed to learn from Vietnam was "No more Vietnams." To many, this meant no military intervention, period. One poll taken shortly before the fall of Saigon reported that only a third of all Americans were willing to support the defense of Berlin militarily. In fact, the only country that a majority of Americans were willing to defend militarily was Canada. Skepticism about military intervention was so pervasive that it achieved the status of a syndrome—the "Vietnam syndrome."[9]

Those who sought to retain America's prerogative to intervene militarily were at pains to distinguish future military actions from

Vietnam. They distinguished these actions by the presence of three factors: clear and achievable objectives; a willingness to use sufficient force to win quickly; and popular support for the mission. Such support might be garnered if the first two criteria were met. Crucial to retaining such support, military strategists now understood, was limited access by the press. The Reagan and Bush administrations demonstrated in circumscribed fashion that military intervention was indeed possible in the wake of Vietnam, undertaking brief and relatively minor actions in Grenada and Panama. Reagan was less successful in Lebanon and Latin America, however. The greatest breakthrough came in the Persian Gulf in 1991, when George Bush proclaimed, the day after a cease-fire was declared, "By God, we've kicked the Vietnam syndrome once and for all." That the president would draw such a conclusion, right or wrong, about a major military engagement almost twenty years after American troops were withdrawn from Vietnam suggests just how palpable that "syndrome" was.[10]

The Vietnam War also bequeathed a powerful set of domestic legacies. The battle between the war's supporters and those who demanded immediate withdrawal divided the nation. Many analysts claim that this debate produced the greatest fissure since the Civil War. It tore at the fabric of society, created deep and lasting divisions, and shattered political unity. In his inaugural address, fifteen years after American troops had been withdrawn from Vietnam, George Bush was still concerned about these divisions, warning Americans that "the final lesson of Vietnam is that no great nation can long afford to be sundered by a memory." Remarking on the reception that Robert McNamara received while attending a conference in Hanoi in 1995, Charles Neu noted that despite the millions of casualties inflicted by the war, "McNamara encountered less hostility in Hanoi than he did traveling around his own country."[11]

The antiwar movement served as catalyst and lightning rod for the divisions that sprang from the war. Adopting some of the techniques used by the civil rights movement, antiwar protesters expanded the boundaries of pluralist participation. That the object of their concern was foreign policy dramatized the insulated nature of decision making in this traditionally elite preserve. It exposed the gulf that lay between the executive foreign policy apparatus and democratic participation, subjecting foreign policy to the vagaries of shifts in public opinion.[12] The antiwar movement also provided a plethora of examples for the emerging New Left critique of American society, adding an edge—or "relevance," in the parlance of the times—to its criticism of foreign policy and the connective tissue of the military-industrial-university complex. That school of thought, built around the work of C. Wright Mills, William Appleman Williams, and David Noble, has influenced American scholarship from the mid-sixties to this day.[13]

Those seeking to influence foreign policy were stalking a moving target as the Vietnam War propelled the executive branch of government toward the "imperial presidency." Such expansion of power occurs with most wars; in fact, Michael Sherry has suggested that what became known as the imperial presidency should really be called the "war presidency." The war that contributed the most to this expansion, of course, was the Cold War, not the one in Vietnam. But besides the body bags that streamed back from Vietnam, two additional factors underscored the emergence of an imperial presidency. The first was Lyndon Johnson's efforts to hide the war. Because Americans at home were not asked to make the kind of sacrifices that had been expected in previous wars—rationing, price and wage controls, tax increases—and because Johnson himself insisted that this was a "limited" war, the extension of the president's unilateral ability to make war seemed less warranted than in past wars. So did the secrecy that surrounded the conflict in Vietnam.[14]

The second factor that highlighted the wartime extension of power was the burgeoning opposition to the substance of executive foreign policy. As Congress responded to the increasingly mainstream opposition to the war, it sought to reassert prerogatives traditionally usurped by presidents during wartime, making the imperial presidency itself an issue, along with the administration's pursuit of an unpopular war. Sidney Milkis points to one of the most profound implications of Vietnam's contribution to the imperial presidency. For decades, Democrats had linked their party's fortunes to programmatic reform, aided and abetted by an expanding presidency. "When this supposition was seemingly violated by the Vietnam War and subsequent developments," Milkis notes, "reformers set out to protect liberal programs from unfriendly executive administration." For liberal Democrats to lead the charge against an overly assertive executive was indeed a new development in the post–New Deal era.[15]

Had the wartime presidents been credible, the imperial presidency might well have escaped relatively unscathed. Unfortunately, they were not. Lies about America's engagement in Vietnam produced a "credibility gap" by Lyndon Johnson's second term in office. Asked in 1989 what junior high school students most needed to know about the Vietnam War, Seymour Hersh responded, "The Pentagon Papers show how Presidents Kennedy and Johnson lied to the American people and to Congress about the origins of the war. I can think of no more important lesson—that we cannot trust our leaders to send us to kill and be killed."[16] Investigative reporters such as Hersh revealed that the fabrications continued, exposing Nixon's lies to his own administration about the secret bombing of Cambodia and bringing to light the massacre at My Lai.

The distrust spread far beyond the presidency itself to virtually all agencies of the government and to institutions in general. Nor was it limited to the more radical fringe of the antiwar movement that imbibed the New Left's critique of the military-industrial-university complex. As was often the case in previous wars, veterans provided an early warning sign of what was to follow in the larger population, proving to be particularly distrustful of their government. Even the Veterans Administration acknowledged that vets reported "greater distrust of institutions" and a "bitterness, disgust and suspicion of those in positions of authority and responsibility." The problem spread far beyond the veracity of institutions and individuals in positions of power. As James Patterson summed it up, "the war undercut the standing of political elites. Nothing did more than Vietnam to subvert the grand expectations that many Americans had developed by 1965 about the capacity of government to deal with public problems. Popular doubt and cynicism about 'the system' and the Washington Establishment lingered long after the men came home." Vietnam was blamed by scholars and the public alike for undermining the basis of public authority. This jaundiced view transcended ideological divisions: whether viewing government from the left or the right, Americans no longer trusted their public officials; their very objectives were discredited.[17]

Watergate stretched the credibility gap and trust in public institutions to the breaking point. But the scandal itself was a product of the poisoned environment created by the conflict in Vietnam and the opposition to it at home. One of the Watergate conspiracy's targets, George McGovern, blames the Vietnam War for its origins. Citing the secret bombing of Cambodia in particular, he claims that Watergate "grew out of the conspiratorial atmosphere, the credibility problems, and the manipulative character of our leaders during the war"—a position sustained by most scholars.[18]

Already buffeted by criticism from the New Left and soon to be challenged by remarkably similar critiques of public authority from the right, liberal leaders struggled to settle the war that broke out within the Democratic party over Vietnam. As E. J. Dionne has noted, liberal Democrats "got the worst of all worlds: on the one hand, they were blamed for a conflict that became 'liberalism's war. . . .' On the other hand, the Democratic Party's close association with the antiwar movement tarred it in the eyes of moderate and conservative voters as the party of military weakness, flag burning, and draft dodging." The cleavage between the "Cold War" wing of the party and the "New Left" wing, epitomized by the riot outside the Democratic convention in 1968, was brought inside the party by McGovern's nomination in 1972. Nixon's landslide victory over McGovern left the Democratic party in a shambles. Although the party's left wing has been muted by the country's swing to the right since the election of Ronald Reagan, the ideological and cultural cleavage created by Vietnam remains a significant fault line today.[19]

As the financial cost of the war was exposed, Lyndon Johnson had to choose between his commitment to domestic reform and the war. He chose the latter. Doris Kearns captured the president's tortured reasoning: "I was bound to be crucified either way I moved," Johnson told Kearns in 1970. "If I left the woman I really loved—the Great Society—in order to get involved with the bitch of a war on the other side of the world, then I would lose everything at home . . . but if I left that war and let the communists take over South Viet Nam, then I would be seen as a coward and my nation would be seen as an appeaser." The war not only drained resources from the Great Society, it played havoc with the economy. It contributed to large budget deficits, which triggered inflation and undermined the dollar in international markets. For the first time since the turn of the century, America began to run trade deficits. By the 1980s, the United States had become a net-debtor nation.[20]

Though more difficult to measure, the cultural legacy of the Vietnam War was as pervasive and persistent as the material one. The war altered some of the fundamental coordinates of American culture. As John Hellmann put it, "On the deepest level, the legacy of Vietnam is the disruption of our story, of our explanation of the past and vision of the future."[21]

This was most apparent in the form that memorials took. Organized by veterans themselves, the national memorial on the Mall in Washington, D.C., has been described as a "black gash of shame" by those used to the more traditional flag-flying and uplifting war monuments. The dark wall that simply lists the names of Americans killed in Vietnam was in fact so controversial that a life-size statue of three GIs was added to satisfy the traditionalists. When compared to the statue commemorating Iwo Jima, however, this compromise seems only to underscore the absence of national unity and self-confidence. As Marilyn Young observed, "these soldiers are flagless and exhausted. They seem to be waiting for something, but the only thing visible in the direction in which they look are the giant slabs with the names of their dead comrades." In the past, war monuments portrayed individuals in their most public guise—personal experience was melded into heroic acts in service to the nation. With the construction of the New York Vietnam Memorial, this tradition was inverted. Here, excerpts from poems and diaries of soldiers who served in Vietnam are carved into a translucent glass wall. The personal trumped the heroic. These memorials provide a final resting place for what Tom Engelhardt calls "victory culture"—a powerful belief in the nation's ultimate triumph over savage enemies threatening the American way of life.[22]

From Legacies to Metaphor

The most enduring legacy of the Vietnam War has been its evolution from a historical event to a metaphor for some of America's most pressing domestic problems. That Vietnam replaced Munich as the operative metaphor in foreign policy after 1970 is well established. The domestic component of Vietnam as metaphor has not been as thoroughly examined. This is not to say that it has been entirely ignored. Norman Podhoretz, for example, wrote that "even before April 30, 1975 . . . Vietnam had become perhaps the most negatively charged political symbol in American history, awaiting only the literal end of the American involvement to achieve its full and final diabolization." Richard Sullivan noted, "The ease with which . . . we use the very word *Vietnam* to register a complex of meanings, devoid for the most part of any cultural or social referents to a particular country or nation or people we might identify with the Vietnamese, is an index of the degree to which the war has been mythologized as an American cultural phenomenon." The Vietnam War has become the "site of struggle over popular memory and cultural meaning."[23]

Legacies are bounded and discrete: they can be measured and studied. Why did America turn away from military engagement? What caused the resurgence of Congress? To the extent that Vietnam or attitudes about Vietnam answer these questions, these trends can be considered part of the legacy of the war. Legacies can be combined with other causal factors. In the case of congressional resurgence, for instance, there was an evolution from policy-based to constituency-based career paths for elected representatives. Because legacies are about causation, they are time-bound. For example, Vietnam had a devastating impact on the prestige of the military. But with the help of Ronald Reagan, and in response to some of the lessons learned in Vietnam, the military rebuilt its image in the 1980s. Considering the treatment of veterans is a good way to distinguish between legacy and metaphor. As we have already noted, veterans *could* serve metaphorical purposes: they symbolized both the will to forget and, later, the determination to remember. And veterans have always been used to convince the next generation of potential soldiers to fulfill their obligation to the state. But the influence of veterans on society could also be measured in more concrete ways, such as by their organized efforts to obtain benefits comparable to those provided after past wars and to achieve the recognition to which they felt entitled. Their success in these endeavors was bounded by competing political interests and such pedestrian but essential considerations as demographics. We can trace this legacy of the war—the rise and fall of veterans' influence—as a discrete historical phenomenon.[24]

Metaphors, on the other hand, have a half-life that is difficult to measure. They endure until replaced by another metaphor. They serve as a "blank screen" that absorbs unrelated concerns and tailors images of subsequent events to fit within its confines. As Jo-Anne Brown has suggested, the very vagueness and multiplicity of a metaphor's meanings can make it a powerful social adhesive. While the meaning of a metaphor is often assumed to be self-evident, each listener in fact connects private meaning to the public symbol. Metaphors thus serve to create a powerful illusion of consensus when in fact multiple meanings exist. Before an event is "metaphorized," it is often seen as the product of a number of social phenomena. But at some point in the process, a transformation occurs. The metaphor itself becomes so powerful as to absorb competing explanations and other possible contributing causes.[25]

The domestic impact of Vietnam is a case in point. Initially, Vietnam was portrayed as the product of a confluence of American institutions and culture. Graham Greene's novel *The Quiet American* is particularly poignant in this regard, anthropomorphizing America's innocence and hubris. An ideological example is the way the war in Vietnam was treated by the New Left. The conflict, which as late as December 1964 was not particularly high on the agenda of the Students for a Democratic Society (SDS), was viewed as a product of "the system": a classic case of the military-industrial-university complex overreaching itself. Student radicals were more concerned about the domestic implications of that system. This was reflected in the SDS's early antiwar slogans, such as "War on Poverty—Not on People" and the famous civil rights slogan "Freedom Now," applied to Vietnam. Even when Johnson began the bombing of North Vietnam in 1965, SDS president Paul Potter did not lose his perspective. The war was merely a product of "the system." Potter told an antiwar rally, "We must name that system. We must name it, describe it, analyze it, understand it and change it. For it is only when that system is changed and brought under control that there can be any hope for stopping the forces that create a war in Vietnam today or a murder in the South tomorrow." Vietnam was becoming both a screen on which to project the New Left's political ideology and a symbol of deep structural problems in American society.[26]

But the power of the Vietnam metaphor soon substituted the

event itself for its causes: Vietnam became the cause of many of America's problems, even though some of the problems it epitomized were antecedent to the war itself. In what can be viewed as a parody of this process, Francis Ford Coppola explained how his attempt to make a film about the Vietnam War evolved into the war itself. Emerging from the Philippine jungle where he had been filming *Apocalypse Now,* the director told a press conference at the Cannes film festival, "My film is not a movie about Vietnam. It is Vietnam. It is what it was really like. It was crazy. And the way we made it was very much like the Americans were in Vietnam. We were in the jungle, there were too many of us. We had access to too much money and too much equipment and little by little, we went insane." Coppola described the arsenal employed to film *Apocalypse:* 1,200 gallons of gasoline consumed in ninety seconds, 2,000 rocket flares, and so on.[27] What had started out as an effort to portray and understand the Vietnam War became, instead, the war itself. Turned into a metaphor, Vietnam ceased to require explanation; rather, it circumscribed other possibilities, and it explained much that followed.

The power of Vietnam as a metaphor for domestic turmoil and decline derives from three interwoven elements: the decline of authority; a new level of conflict; and the fragmentation of national identity. The genealogy of these components is apparent from our review of the legacies of Vietnam. Metaphors are not fabricated out of thin air. The Vietnam metaphor bears a close resemblance to many of the consequences produced by that war. The conflict in Vietnam, the metaphor instructs, destroyed the trust that Americans had placed in their president and the authority of government institutions in general. Measured by public polling data, the level of mistrust in government nearly tripled in the decade after 1964. Vietnam (and to a lesser degree Watergate) is blamed for much of this decline. Vietnam shattered faith in experts and undermined the authority of all elites who pursued ambitious policy agendas. Since the Vietnam War, Americans have remained skeptical of their government, suspicious of their political leaders. They have also, the Vietnam metaphor suggests, remained divided in ways that seemingly defy resolution. During the war itself, militant actions and civil disobedience—whether dodging the draft or burning the flag—created a cultural divide that has still not narrowed. What distinguished these conflicts from previous social divisions was their seemingly intractable nature: antiwar protesters rejected pragmatic compromise and demanded that decisions be made on moral grounds, not on the basis of politics as usual. Vietnam threatened to "destroy the bonds which held us together." Like the war itself, this conflict seemed interminable. The loss in Vietnam, the fact that communism remained at bay despite the loss, and the exposure of America's exceptionalist position as myth fragmented the nation's identity, the metaphor implies. Rather than embracing the reflexive patriotism that had held the country together for much of the century, Americans increasingly wondered just what it meant to be an American. It was no longer a rhetorical question. Their story disrupted, Americans sought to pick up the pieces or craft a new one.[28]

Hollywood played a crucial role in projecting the Vietnam metaphor onto screens across the nation. Video images were particularly convincing, since that is how much of the public received its news about the war in the first place. Students of the media are quick to point out that only a small percentage of the news broadcast about Vietnam featured "bang-bang" footage. Perhaps because of this, those shots that did show actual fighting made a lasting impression. What's more, some of that footage was staged, since the enemy's attacks rarely accommodated camera people. The "television war" prepared Americans visually for the more elaborately staged scenes that they would later view in movie theaters. Vietnam on video seemed like the real thing.[29]

At first, films followed the same pattern of denial about Vietnam as the American public. There were no major releases featuring the war between John Wayne's *The Green Berets* in 1968 and *Coming*

Home and *The Deer Hunter* in 1978. As one film critic put it, "A war that traumatized and divided American society was not a logical topic for popular entertainment." *The Green Berets* had been made in the grand tradition of war films that disseminate the patriotic message Washington sought to broadcast. The lesson that Hollywood drew from the movie's poor reception was that this form was not appropriate for this war. Subsequent films either referred to Vietnam metaphorically or took the politics out of the war. By the mid-eighties, Hollywood had overcome its aversion. Twelve years after Saigon fell, it was hard to book a room in Bangkok, so great was the demand by American crews shooting Vietnam films. There are now more than 400 feature films about the Vietnam War.[30]

Treating Vietnam metaphorically contributed to the impression that the war was behind everything—or at least everything bad—that was happening to America. In his essay "Hollywood and Vietnam," Michael Anderegg writes that "some would say that a Vietnam allegory underlies virtually every significant American film released from the mid-sixties to the mid-seventies, from *Bonnie and Clyde* (1967) and *Night of the Living Dead* (1968) to *Ulzana's Raid* (1972) and *Taxi Driver* (1976)." By 1978 Hollywood was ready to take on the war directly. But it did so by focusing on the personal anguish of the individual soldier. There are no counterparts to the numerous World War II films that focused on the command level. Making such a film would have required engagement with the larger political picture and purpose of the war. Rather than loyalty to nation or a set of ideals associated with the nation, the emphasis of most films about the Vietnam War is on situational loyalty—to other soldiers, for instance. This depoliticization severed the major arteries of causation—whether the State Department's view or "the system" as analyzed by Paul Potter—in many of the films about Vietnam. According to Hollywood, Vietnam happened the way "shit happens."[31]

Short on how we got there, Hollywood has been extraordinarily long on how we get out of Vietnam. The need to heal and reconcile is a major theme that runs through the films, literature, and many of the cultural artifacts produced about Vietnam in the last twenty years. Both *The Deer Hunter* and *Coming Home* are about veterans who, despite their torturous experiences and difficulty forgetting, ultimately move beyond the war. For some characters, such as Rambo in *First Blood, Part II,* only rewriting the conclusion of the war will suffice. When asked to return to Vietnam on a secret mission to obtain photographic evidence that prisoners of war are still being held, Rambo utters the famous line, "Do we get to win this time?" "It's precisely that bummer of an ending," film critic J. Hoberman observed, "that's left us with a compulsion to remake—well if not history, then at least the movie. The impossible longing for a satisfactory conclusion tempts each Vietnam film to sell itself as definitive." Before reconciliation occurs in a film, however, the horrors of Vietnam are relentlessly rehearsed and in some instances magnified.[32]

Accumulated images of horror conveyed through the popular media have fortified the Vietnam metaphor and underscored the connections between the loss of authority, a different order of conflict, and the fragmented national identity that all need to be repaired or reconciled in the wake of the tragedy. *Coming Home,* the story of a legless, embittered vet who is reintegrated into society because he is able to fall in love, carries the saccharine message that "love heals." Nevertheless, when *Time* reviewed the film, it characterized it as "one long howl of pain." Commenting on the popularization of Vietnam as a subject or at least backdrop for television shows, Peter Martin noted that "as much as the culture industries strive to popularize the Vietnam war, in the process they cannot avoid touching on the very issues that made the war a bitterly divisive and controversial event in the first place." The quest to reconcile, in other words, has consolidated the assault on American consensus that Vietnam has come to stand for.[33]

The Vietnam metaphor was not confined to the screen. Scholars also "metaphorized" Vietnam and soon adopted it as a shorthand for the sixties. Terry Anderson, for instance, writes, "Philosophers often wonder: what determines change, what is the engine of history?" His answer for one decade, at least, is clear: "The Vietnam War became the engine of the sixties." Others have labeled the war a boundary-altering event and a symbol for domestic unrest. Few have argued with Barbara Tischler's assertion that "the Vietnam War became the most important cultural symbol in this country from the mid-1960s until the withdrawal of American forces in 1973 as dress and style increasingly represented views on the war itself, the government, and authority in general." The Vietnam metaphor cannibalized the structural critique of America offered by New Left thinkers. It came to embody, rather than explain, the nation's problems. If dramatic conflicts such as urban rioting and the demands of Black Power could be overshadowed by Vietnam, there was little chance that more subtle changes, such as the evolution of group politics or the emergence of a global economy, might be linked to the turmoil the nation now associated with Vietnam.[34]

The war and the movement against it seemed to devour every other concern. It took over the student movement. It strained the finances of the Great Society. Even the powerful civil rights movement became embroiled in it. The violence of Vietnam was brought home to the Democratic national convention in 1968. The war consumed the presidency and monopolized foreign policy as the quest to assure America's credibility ultimately undermined the confidence of the nation's allies. And there could be no doubt that the country had changed dramatically during the Vietnam period. By the 1970s America had lost its sense of common purpose, according to William Chafe. "A new era had dawned, lacking the confidence, optimism, and sense of national purpose that had dominated the immediate postwar period." The Vietnam metaphor had engulfed, and certainly seemed to explain, many of these changes.[35]

Vietnam in Context

By the 1980s, the Vietnam metaphor itself was a quagmire. It had absorbed so many of the features associated with the sixties that, like *Apocalypse Now*, that decade was in danger of *becoming* the Vietnam War. The Vietnam metaphor has skewed our historical understanding of the 1960s by obscuring a number of less visible influences in that period.[36] Four causal factors that have little to do with Vietnam help explain the challenge to authority, the heightened political conflict, and the fragmented national identity. While this is not the place for an exhaustive review of the sixties, exploring these four themes is the way to begin extricating the explanations for the changes that took place in America from the disproportionate influence of the Vietnam metaphor. When placed alongside Vietnam and in some instances antecedent to Vietnam, they help to account for where we are today.

The civil rights revolution is by far the most visible of these four factors. It is also the one that is best integrated into the scholarship on this period. Dependent upon the courageous actions of individuals during much of the 1950s, the struggle for racial equality burst upon the public scene in the 1960s as a powerful social movement that reshaped laws and attitudes. Besides ending Jim Crow in the South, the civil rights movement led millions to embrace Black Power, contributed to the rioting that shook the very foundation of social order in many cities, evolved into a permanent lobby within the federal government for the expansion of civil rights, provided a model that led to the adoption of similar techniques by other minorities and by women, and was instrumental in the extension of rights and the means for securing those rights to millions of immigrants.

Although the civil rights movement and the leadership of articulate African American spokesmen such as Martin Luther King Jr. and Malcolm X have received extensive popular and scholarly attention, some of the more subtle yet influential legacies of the quest for civil rights have been all but neglected. Take, for instance, the revolution in immigration policy that was set in motion (quite unintentionally) by the 1965 legislation that ended the quota system designed to ensure that the majority of immigrants would come from western and northern Europe. By the 1980s, only a tenth of all immigrants to the United States were from Europe. As Peter Skerry has argued, the mechanisms through which immigrants mobilized politically were radically altered. The predominant model was now a "racialized" one. "This reflects a more general tendency in our political culture," Skerry contends, "such that we now have one dominant way of discussing and analyzing disadvantage: in terms of race. Yet this profound change in the context in which immigration policy gets made, and in which immigrants learn to define their goals and interests, has gone largely unexamined." Another legislative change, the inclusion of discrimination on the basis of sex in Title VII of the Civil Rights Act of 1964 as part of the mandate of the Equal Employment Opportunity Commission—an amendment supported in large part by conservative Southern Democrats, who sought to water down the authority of the EEOC—eventually contributed to a significant alteration in employment patterns for women. Arguably, the greatest gains achieved by those who sought to expand civil rights protection occurred after much of the marching had stopped, fueled by increased voting, active lobbying, and the heightened consciousness on a day-to-day basis of individuals who believed that equal rights—or at least more nearly equal rights—were in fact within their grasp.[37]

The struggle for equal rights undermined authority in this country at the most fundamental level. The civil rights movement waged war on the racial and gendered hierarchy that had prevailed since the nation's founding. Each victory disrupted the distribution of social and political authority and power. Those who argue that Vietnam was the most divisive event since the Civil War should at least limit their claims to the white middle class. Race has always been a profound dividing line in America.[38] This division was underscored and reinforced in the 1960s, first by the attention that was focused on racial inequality, next by the movement to celebrate racial pride. The urban rioting that occurred primarily among African Americans in the sixties hardened the racial divide. Although equal opportunity was closely associated with America's national identity, the demand that the gap between promise and reality be closed fragmented America's sense of purpose far more than it unified the nation. The counterreaction to greater demands for racial and gender justice has further divided the nation and complicated the collective project of establishing a new national identity.

A second factor that should be added to Vietnam in our quest for a more balanced understanding of the sixties is the further extension of pluralism. The civil rights revolution, of course, established the legitimacy of racial and gendered differences—challenging the hierarchy that placed whiteness and men on top—and thus advanced the cause of social and cultural pluralism. Another variant of pluralism was transformed in the sixties: what I will call political pluralism, or simply group politics. Political pluralism had been the American political science theory of choice since the early twentieth century; with the work of David Truman, it had achieved a near-hegemonic hold on that discipline by the early 1960s. But, as critics from E. E. Schattschneider to Theodore Lowi noted, group influence was in reality available to a far smaller portion of the polity than the theory suggested. In the 1960s, the number and variety of interest groups participating in politics exploded. "Public interest" lobbies led the charge. Many of these grew out of the social movements of the sixties and imbibed the New Left's suspicion of authority.[39]

At the same time, the expansion of the professions, led in part by the federal government's investment in the production of experts and its pursuit of ambitious agendas, forged a symbiotic relationship between the professions and the federal government that yielded a pattern of political power that I have dubbed the "proministrative" state, for its synthesis of professional and administrative capacity. The professions—now operating with technologies that required resources that the voluntary sector could not match, ranging from particle accelerators to space telescopes, and seeking to master vast data sets, whether epidemiological or sociological—required federal resources. They also needed the political and legal authority to set their ideas in motion, whether the issue was smoking or teenage pregnancy. The federal government, on the other hand, benefited from the prestige and authority wielded by the professions after World War II. It also turned to these experts as a major source of guidance in policy areas ranging from military to environmental.[40]

Prominstrators preferred to work in insulated forums, often protected by claims of "national security" or the esoteric nature of their work. But because their programs were producer-driven, not consumer-driven (householders didn't, for example, demand that the electricity coming out of their sockets be generated by nuclear power), professionals and the agencies that housed them teamed up to "sell" their programs to the public. The necessity for going public—often with spectacular promises of benefits to follow—clashed directly with the preference for insulated consultation and debate. Expert authority, in fact, had always been highly dependent upon maintaining the illusion of consensus in public, no matter how fierce the debate behind the scenes.

Besides the need to sell the programs, a number of tendencies inherent in the dynamic of prominstrative politics pushed expert debate out of insulated forums into more public arenas. The most important of these was specialization, both professional and organizational. Another was the interdisciplinary approach required to implement complex programs. A final tendency was the proliferation of experts, in large part generated by the prominstrators themselves. Political actors previously excluded from esoteric debates now found it far easier to hire their own experts, since there was a surfeit of them. Those who could now participate in policy debates brought a host of new political perspectives with them. Interest groups that linked all three levels of America's governmental system (federal, state, and local) were often the critical agents in this process: they spread debate from the institutional arenas to broader audiences. The internal dynamic of prominstrative politics was magnified by a rapidly expanding and more assertive press corps.[41] The cacophony of competing expert opinions eroded the special advantages held by prominstrators at the outset and forced programs toward more traditional bases of support among interest groups or parties. The simultaneous erosion of the experts' public consensus across a spectrum of policy areas undermined the public's general confidence in experts, regardless of their field. It also lessened confidence in the government programs that had relied so heavily on expert agendas. This was, indeed, an explanation for the decline of authority quite different from that contained in the Vietnam metaphor.

The combination of this enlarged pluralist base and publicly contentious professional community provided a social base from which controversial issues could be pursued indefinitely. Groups that lost the battle in Congress could take the fight to administrative forums. Failure there often led to the courts. Expert forums, which had once had the first and last word about esoteric matters, were now just one voice among many. As Hugh Heclo has observed, the policymaking system was asked to do more at the same time that public officials were trusted less.[42]

Heclo characterizes this system as "radically pluralized" and "postmodern"—in large part because of the actors' distrust of the very institutions that they relied upon to implement their programs. Along with the "postmodern" elements in today's pluralism, its capacious range explains a great deal. "Radically pluralistic" politics is what you get when you multiply the players, diversify their interests, provide each side access to scientific authorities, and put cultural issues and questions about process on the table along with economic ones. Whatever the root causes, Heclo's description of "radically pluralistic" politics distills many of the features often attributed to the Vietnam metaphor. The further extension of political pluralism undermined authority: "Confidence in administrative discretion, expertise, and professional independence," Heclo argues, "had to be replaced by continuous public scrutiny, hard-nosed advocacy, strict timetables, and stringent standards for prosecuting the policy cause in question." More fully realized political pluralism is also confrontational and divisive. Group leaders, required to mobilize supporters behind the "cause" and often relying on media campaigns to do so, have little leeway for compromise. Heclo is most eloquent on the implications of sixties-style group politics for the nation's identity. "The now-adult, divided, radically pluralistic Sixties generation was taking over the reins of power. More than that, they were leading an inchoate debate on what political vision of the world could have authority over the nation. In effect, the search was on for a higher public moral order in a policy culture denying there could be any such thing."[43]

The final two factors offered for consideration return us to the world of international affairs. The fierce debate about Vietnam—both during the war and after—masked two of the most significant developments in the last forty years: America's participation in a global economy and the attenuation of the Cold War. By 1975, America's role in the world economy had shifted. Exposure to the global economy, symbolized by the first oil crisis of 1973, soon subjected core American industries such as automobile manufacturing and steel to intense pressure from foreign competitors. Louis Galambos has written about the ways in which the Vietnam War obscured this problem and cost the United States a decade in recognizing it and beginning to respond to it. He makes it clear that the war did not cause this transition; it was happening anyway. The Vietnam War also overshadowed changes within the Soviet Union and interrupted the trend toward détente, which can be traced back to the early 1960s. The path out of the Cold War hardly ran in a straight line—in part because of the cul-de-sac of Vietnam. Nevertheless, a case can be made that America's relations with the Soviet

Union had begun to thaw long before Nixon officially declared détente.[44]

Exposure to the global economy and the thaw in the Cold War affected Americans' attitudes toward authority and national identity in similar ways, though for different reasons. The global economy raised doubts about the ability of nation-states to control crucial variables affecting their citizens' lives. One of the major legacies of World War II had been the firm establishment of federal responsibility for the nation's economic health. The recognition that Americans were competing in a global economy challenged the federal government's authority in this sphere, much as the Great Depression had raised questions about the ability of state and local governments to perform a host of services. As economist Philip Cerny notes, "This new global transformation has gravely challenged the capacity of the state to provide effective governance not only of financial markets themselves but of economic affairs generally." The emergence of détente in the mid-sixties undermined national authority in a different way. Americans had granted the national security state historically disproportionate amounts of discretion and power because of the perceived threat from the Soviet Union. As that threat was reduced, many began to question the need for such blanket dispensations of authority.[45]

When it came to national identity, the economy and bipolar relations also stimulated similar trends for different reasons. America's privileged position in the world economy had strongly reinforced the notion of American exceptionalism. As that position was challenged, so was the exceptionalist component of American's national identity. By the early 1960s, the Cold War had become a part of the nation's identity. Countless rifts and differences had been papered over in the interest of presenting a united front to the enemy. As the Cold War thawed, Americans were confronted with the challenge of defining for themselves just what it meant to be American without the framework of external threat that had played such a crucial role in that definition over the past two decades.[46] It is no accident that when Ronald Reagan turned to the task of restoring the nation's confidence, he did so by reviving the perceived threat from the "evil empire."

There is a reason that the civil rights revolution, the further extension of pluralist access to experts and political power, the globalization of the economy, and the end of the Cold War are not frequently associated with the decline of authority, a different order of conflict, and the fragmentation of national identity. The changes wrought by the civil rights movement are considered one of the great triumphs of American history, symbolized by the celebration of Martin Luther King Jr.'s birthday as a national holiday. Squaring real pluralist access with long-held beliefs about political pluralism must also be registered as a victory for liberal democracy, though it is a less celebrated one. Few would argue with the benefits derived from ending the Cold War, though some are still looking for the "peace dividend." And despite the heated debate over the North American Free Trade Agreement (NAFTA) and concern over the stability of the ruble, both political parties seem to have embraced America's explicit entry into the global economy as the next frontier for Americans to conquer. In other words, the structural changes rooted in the 1960s that I have enumerated range from triumphant to positive. Arrayed against these, tragically trapped in its rancid metaphorical quagmire, is Vietnam. It is unambiguously negative. Because we are uncomfortable with the idea that something as good for the nation as the civil rights revolution or the end of the Cold War carries costs, we have assigned these costs to a phenomenon that clearly cost a bundle—Vietnam. The metaphor mentality ultimately leads to bumper-sticker slogans such as "No more Vietnams." A historically better informed explication of America's problems can't be reduced to "No more rights," "No more participation," "More bipolar global conflict," or "No more cheap consumer goods."

The massive challenges that we face—reestablishing authority to perform tasks essential to the public good, ensuring that disputes are mediated and reach closure, defining a sense of national purpose—are too easily attributed to a particularly evil event or conspiracy of events. Surely they couldn't be the flip side of some of our most compelling achievements? The fact that Vietnam is "over there" (geographically) and "back then" (temporally) makes it all the more suitable to carry this burden, and it seems all the easier to "put it behind us." Separating the evil from the good is one of the functions fulfilled by the litany of metaphors that "define" the sixties—JFK's assassination, Watergate, and Vietnam.

Conclusion

Metaphors are bad for history. They are good at evoking collective memory and contributing to a sense of shared experience, which we as a society are in great need of. They are also good at pinpointing the most pressing issues faced by a society—in this case the decline of authority, the rising level of conflict and the difficulty of reaching closure on disputes, and the fragmentation of national identity. Metaphors achieve this, however, by relying on an emotional shorthand that obscures complex causal relationships. The most significant consequence in this case is the failure to recognize the tradeoffs entailed by social change. If we had a magic eraser, we would gladly efface the Vietnam War from American history. (Indeed, this was the first response to Vietnam by politicians and filmmakers alike.) Doing so would, if we subscribe to the Vietnam metaphor, also restore much that has been lost along the way: authority, unity, and national identity. If, however, these public assets were eroded not only by the legacy of Vietnam but also by the quest for civil rights, the further extension of political pluralism, the end of the Cold War, and the embracing of a global economy, many of us would not bother to remove the plastic wrap from that eraser. Acknowledging the negative consequences that were integral to positive developments makes it far more difficult to externalize obstacles that remain in our path. They can't simply be exorcised, attributed to the conspiracy of a few evil men, or blamed on a misguided mind-set. They are interwoven into the fabric of our society and the very things that we value the most.

Several recent presidents have actively sought to deflate and replace the Vietnam metaphor. They have done so for instrumental reasons—to free up military options that had been stifled by the foreign policy implications of the Vietnam metaphor. It is time to assault the domestic component of the metaphor as well. Those of us who subscribe to the slogan "No more Vietnams," however, would be wise to ask a few questions before plunging in. How did the Vietnam metaphor grow to be so powerful? What were the political bases of those who nurtured it? What, precisely, was the relationship between popular images of Vietnam and scholarly treatments of its legacy? How was each influenced by the media? Demystifying the Vietnam metaphor and placing Vietnam in its proper historical context will allow us to achieve a richer historical understanding of our recent past. It will pave the way toward acceptance of the full panoply of consequences that accompany the benefits bestowed by a democratizing and increasingly globalized society.

The most significant of these consequences is the return of the American state to a more traditional relationship to civil society. Artificially emboldened, inflated, and insulated by the historical confluence of World War II and the Cold War, by the remarkable degree of discretion and influence enjoyed by proministrators, and by the exceptional position that the American economy enjoyed in comparison to the rest of the world, the nation-state demanded and received a unique degree of respect and loyalty.[47] Nothing demonstrates the relative power of the American state better than its decision to tackle head-on the nation's most intractable problem: racial discrimination. About the time that America committed hundreds of thousands of troops to Vietnam—*and partly as a result of that decision*—the foundation for this political constellation began to shift. By the time the last Americans were plucked by helicopter from the roof of the Saigon embassy, the consequences of this shift had become apparent to all. The causes were, however, after a brief period of collective amnesia, too easily conflated with Vietnam.

One final assault on Vietnam—this one directed at the domestic element in the Vietnam metaphor—will allow us to recognize the permanent changes in the nature of authority, unity, and identity that have occurred and the degree to which these changes are intertwined with some of the most valuable benefits resulting from the causal factors outlined above. This is not to minimize the importance of these priceless, if intangible, national goods. It may be, however, that they are no longer to be guaranteed by a strong central government. The partial fulfillment of the dream of pluralist participation—both social/cultural and political—has eroded the platforms that afforded policymakers the discretion to maintain stable regimes of regulation and programmatic control. This erosion has undermined the legitimacy of the central government from within. The end of the Cold War and the increasing significance of economic decisions made beyond our borders have undermined the legitimacy of the central government from without. The legacies of Vietnam have contributed to this process, first creating and then helping discredit the imperial presidency, for instance; stimulating direct participation in the political process by millions, adding to the pluralist chorus; and demonstrating that even an embarrassing loss in Vietnam did little to undermine America's national security. But it was hardly the war that started these structural changes, nor could it direct or contain them.

As we integrate these structural changes in the future, we must return to a variety of institutions that have proven more enduring in American history than a strong central government. The list could not be more familiar: family, geographic community, profession or occupational association, religious denomination, and interest groups. If we return, however, we must continue to honor the commitment to pluralist participation. It was the breach in that commitment that discredited so many of these institutions in the early 1960s. This is not to argue that we should abandon the federal government. It remains the only institution likely to enforce the procedural equity that I am calling for. It will also take on an enhanced role as negotiator for American interests in the global marketplace. Where competing domestic interests are able to reach uneasy agreements, the federal government can contribute to the stability of such compromises, as it can enforce their provisions. It must continue to serve as a catalyst for the stimulation of expertise and knowledge. And, of course, it remains the guardian of our national security.

But, returning to its historical role, the federal government will most likely follow the dictates of civil society in initiating new policies, rather than taking the lead itself. Building support for these policies, even if it means embracing interest group politics, is a task to which those determined to reverse the growing social inequality must turn their attention. The ultimate legacy of Vietnam embraces not only the neoconservative lesson that the state exceeded its authority and its capacity, but a pluralist lesson as well: even in the field of foreign policy, the state ultimately yields to mobilized interests. This suggests that the opportunity to use the state for progressive ends still exists. In a "radically pluralized" environment, however, realizing the opportunity is no small challenge.

Preparing *Not* to Refight the Last War

The Impact of the Vietnam War on the U.S. Military

■

GEORGE C. HERRING

I am often asked how I came to devote much of my career to the study of the Vietnam War. I always respond that I don't have a good answer. It just happened.

I was one of that lucky post–World War II generation too young to serve in Korea, too old to serve in Vietnam. I first became conscious of Vietnam as an eighteen-year-old college sophomore during the spring of 1954, fearing that if the United States intervened to save the French at Dien Bien Phu, I might be called to arms.

That did not happen, of course; but, like other males of my generation, I faced a military obligation. Because I had no clue what I wanted to do with my life and because I did not want to be drafted into the Army, I entered the Navy's Officer Candidate School. Some of my college and OCS classmates who went on to military careers served in Vietnam. I did a short tour in the Navy and in 1960 entered graduate school at the University of Virginia.

Growing up in the Cold War era, I was keenly interested in foreign policy and things military, and I early decided to concentrate on diplomatic and military history. During my graduate school days, I was, I suspect, no more conscious than most other Americans of the steadily escalating conflict in Vietnam. I do remember vividly the picture of the Buddhist monk engulfed in flames in summer 1963, the Tonkin Gulf incident, and the election of 1964.

It was only after I began teaching at Ohio University in the fall of 1965 that I, like the rest of the country, became connected to Vietnam. Teaching courses in the history of U.S. foreign policy, I found myself in the midst of an increasingly heated debate on what was now a war, and I began to educate myself on the subject. What I found, probing beneath the surface even just a bit, was so blatantly at odds with the official view and the myopic and unhistorical view presented in the popular media that I could not but look at the war differently. These early historical explorations aroused a curiosity that has remained acute for nearly thirty-five years.

During my time at Ohio University and, after 1969, at the University of Kentucky, Vietnam came to absorb all of us. It was always in the forefront; in classes, the discussion invariably turned to it, no matter what the day's topic. I recall impassioned discussions with students facing the draft and with returned veterans who would admit their service only behind closed doors. In the spring of 1973, I taught my first course on the war, a seminar in which roughly half the students had served in Vietnam, half had protested the war, and some had done both. It was among the most powerful teaching experiences of my life.

Shortly after the fall of Saigon, I wrote a brief essay on the war. I was going to call it "America's Longest War," but the editor did not like that title, so we called it "Vietnam: An American Ordeal." I found the experience of giving the war a history so challenging that I proposed to Professor Robert Divine a book for his America in Crisis series. He was a bit skeptical at first, since the war was so close and the nation so disposed to forget it. But his initial caution turned to enthusiastic support. I spent the years 1975 to 1979 absorbed in the book. I had planned to finish it and go on to something else. Instead, for the next twenty years I continued to spend much of my time studying and teaching about the war. It has been a moving and at times emotionally wrenching experience to witness the hold it continues to have on the nation and especially on those individuals directly affected by it. It has been fascinating as a historian to observe and at times participate in the ongoing and still-heated debate on the war's meaning and lessons—of which the essay that follows is a small part.

■

Toward the latter part of the conflict in Vietnam, journalist Ward Just overheard a senior U.S. officer snarl, "I'll be damned if I permit the United States Army, its institutions, its doctrine, and its traditions to be destroyed just to win this lousy war."[1] As it turned out, of course, the United States did not win that "lousy war." And despite the best efforts of the above-quoted officer and presumably others, the institutions, doctrine, and traditions of all the military services were severely shaken, if not destroyed, in the process of waging it.

The Vietnam War had a profound impact on a once-proud U.S. military establishment, calling into question its conviction, born of its decisive role in two world wars, that it was invincible; challenging, as perhaps nothing before in its history, its faith that the massive application of force was the solution to military problems. Precisely because the war's impact was so great, the armed services could not avoid dealing with the Vietnam experience, as the rest of American society seemed content to do in the immediate postwar years. Military leaders engaged their respective services in an intensive and searching self-analysis that produced a veritable revolution in organization, recruitment, training, education, and doctrine. The Vietnam War thus significantly reshaped the U.S. military.

In another, perhaps more fundamental sense, the military did not deal with Vietnam at all. Many of those responsible for rebuilding military institutions concluded that failure in Vietnam had been the result not of their way of doing things but rather of restrictions imposed on them by civilian leaders. Vietnam thus had little if any impact on postwar military doctrine. Those officers who assumed top leadership positions in the 1980s and 1990s also steadfastly opposed going to war except under the most favorable circumstances—circumstances, obviously, distinctly different from those of Vietnam. The Persian Gulf War vindicated the post-Vietnam military reforms and in some ways exorcised the demons of Vietnam. Within the U.S. military establishment and especially in civil-military relations, however, the effects of that war still linger, with uncertain implications for the future.

I

Long before the last U.S. combat troops departed Vietnam, the once-mighty U.S. military machine had begun to break down. As early as 1971, an expert on military affairs reported that by "every conceivable indicator" the forces remaining in Vietnam were in "a state of approaching collapse."[2] The signs were obvious even to those senior officers who would have preferred to ignore them. A pervasive breakdown of discipline manifested itself in such relatively innocent things as the hippie-like appearance of GIs in the field—the wearing of long hair, love beads, and peace symbols. It was also apparent in the refusal of fighting men to wear helmets in combat and in the promiscuous throwing of grenades. By this time in the war, GIs were as likely to question as to obey orders, and they were less willing to risk their lives in combat. Officers seemed intimidated by troublemakers, and tolerated what Colin Powell later called "outrageous behavior." AWOL and desertion rates rose dramatically. In both the Army and the Marines, individual soldiers and indeed entire units sometimes refused to go into battle, and officers and men cut deals to undertake "search and evade" missions that would keep them out of harm's way. More serious yet was an epidemic of "fragging" incidents—deliberate efforts, usually on the part of enlisted men, to get rid of unpopular or overly aggressive officers by rolling fragmentation grenades into their quarters or clubs.[3]

Drug abuse skyrocketed in the last years of the war. It is impossible to arrive at reliable figures, but a random sample of GIs leaving

South Vietnam in September 1971 revealed that 67 percent had at least experimented with marijuana and 45 percent with hard drugs. Of the 2,500 soldiers evacuated for medical reasons in September 1971, 55 percent were drug abusers rather than battle casualties.[4] Drug use does not appear to have been widespread in the field or to have hampered combat operations, but it was pervasive among support troops and in rear areas.

Throughout all the services and at military installations around the world, racial tensions mounted. The military was the most racially integrated of all American institutions, but African Americans still had not made it into the upper echelons in large numbers. They complained that the system of military justice was skewed against them. Their demands were increasingly militant, a demeanor that was provoked by deeply ingrained racist attitudes among whites and that in turn exposed such attitudes. Racial tensions were generally kept in check in combat situations, but the rear areas seethed. Blacks and whites voluntarily resegregated themselves off duty, and such loaded symbols as Confederate flags and Black Power salutes provoked open conflict.

At best ambivalent in the early days of U.S. involvement, GI attitudes toward the South Vietnamese grew openly hostile as the war ground toward its agonizing end. As morale disintegrated after the Tet Offensive of 1968, Americans increasingly vented their frustration on their nominal allies. Soldiers fired weapons at civilians, hurled rocks and cans at villagers, and drove vehicles in life-threatening ways. "Many armies have dealt harshly with enemy populations," journalist Jonathan Schell wrote in 1970, "but ours certainly is one of the first to deal so harshly with its allies." The most notorious example, of course, and the one that made obvious the breakdown of the Army, was the massacre of 504 Vietnamese civilians by an American company at the village of My Lai in the spring of 1968. The incident and its subsequent cover-up made clear to senior officers who had long kept their heads in the sand that they faced a major crisis.[5]

The causes of the breakdown now seem clear. Any military establishment is a reflection of the society that creates it, and the servicemen brought with them to Vietnam and other military posts the drug problems and racial tensions that wracked the United States. The permissiveness that marked the youth culture of the 1960s carried over into a lack of respect for authority in the military. The length of the war caused growing problems, and after 1968, the obvious fact that the nation had abandoned any thought of winning could not help but affect morale. Boredom and restlessness pervaded rear areas, while combat was at once "dangerous and seemingly devoid of success." No one wanted to be the last American to die in a cause that was obviously lost.[6]

The way the war was fought contributed decisively to the military breakdown. The manpower pool was sharply limited by President Lyndon Johnson's refusal to mobilize the reserves and by a grossly inequitable selective service system that provided a safety net to the best and brightest of American youth. At the same time, the expansion of the war after 1965, the one-year tour, and a high casualty rate created escalating demands for more GIs. Draft boards and recruiting officers lowered their standards, and the services took growing numbers of "foxhole fillers"—less and less well qualified individuals who caused more and more problems.[7] Pressured to fill slots, they rushed troops to Vietnam without the training and preparation necessary to deal with an increasingly difficult situation. The necessity of creating from scratch an entirely new supply of junior officers and noncoms had especially serious consequences for discipline and morale.[8]

The services contributed to their own problems. An Army War College study commissioned by Army Chief of Staff Gen. William C. Westmoreland after the My Lai exposé concluded that an absence of leadership had produced predictable results. In a damning indictment, the study found that "careerism" and "ticket-punching" had replaced the traditional ethics of the officer. Increasingly bureaucratized management practices, the peculiar dynamics of a limited war, and the one-year tour and even more frequent rotation of officers destroyed unit cohesion and put the emphasis on career advancement rather than performance. The bureaucracy's voracious appetite for numbers, a result of the computer age and the managerial revolution instituted at the Pentagon by Secretary of Defense Robert S. McNamara, led the services to focus on what could be quantified rather than the more abstract and elusive concept of leadership. Officers thus concentrated on the trivial and the short-term rather than more important and longer-term matters. Incompetence and its cover-up became standard operating procedures. Shocked by the study, Westmoreland labeled it a "masterpiece" and promptly restricted its circulation to the Army's top officers.[9]

The fall of Saigon in April 1975 had a devastating effect on officers throughout the military establishment. "I grieved as though I had lost a member of my family," a senior officer later recalled, and the harsh reality of failure and defeat left many officers angry and embittered.[10] Some sensibly recognized that even the vast power of the United States had limits. Many more felt betrayed by a civilian leadership that, they alleged, had forced them to fight with one hand tied behind their back. Some complained that the hostility of the media, the antiwar movement, and Congress had snatched defeat from the jaws of victory. Many officers left the service in anger. Some stayed and turned their attention to the seemingly more pressing—and more manageable—problem of the Soviet threat in Europe.[11]

II

Among those who stayed, some officers dedicated their careers to restoring a shattered military to a position of respect and effectiveness, and between 1975 and 1985 the services implemented a series of major reforms. Some were instituted voluntarily; others were imposed by outside authority. Most were based squarely on perceived lessons of Vietnam. The results were little short of revolutionary.

Well before the end of the war, all of the services began to put their respective houses in order, in the process instituting changes that went to the very heart of traditional military culture. The first step, of course, was to restore discipline and order, and here tough measures were often used. The Marines initially dealt with troublemakers in ways that seem almost stereotypical, kicking them out through administrative discharges.[12] At installations across the world, Powell later recalled, Army officers sought to regain control by making clear to soldiers that "I'm in charge and you ain't." Even then, it was the end of the decade before a semblance of order was restored in each of these services.[13]

But the changes went much deeper. Chief of Naval Operations (CNO) Adm. Elmo R. Zumwalt Jr. sought to adapt his service to changing times—and to boost reenlistments—by such reforms as providing more shore time for sailors, liberalizing provisions for liberty and leave, and eliminating what he later called "chickenshit" and "Mickey Mouse" regulations. The Navy also sought to address its deeply entrenched racial problems by broadening opportunities for minorities, establishing councils to discuss racial issues, and placing in Naval Exchange stores items used by African Americans. A new generation of officers tried to "recast the cultural and social mores of the Army to make them relevant to a new generation of Americans." In the process, they "gored some of the Army's most sacred cows," instituting the eight-hour day and five-day week, eliminating Saturday morning inspections, getting rid of the dreaded KP, permitting long hair, replacing open barracks with two-person rooms, and even putting beer machines in barracks.[14]

In the aftermath of Vietnam, the nation changed dramatically the way troops were raised and mobilized. One of the most fundamental of the post-Vietnam military reforms, the All-Volunteer Force, was rammed down the throats of senior officers. The Nixon administration instituted the All-Volunteer Force in 1973 because of the rampant unpopularity of the draft, a direct result of the war. Army leaders saw the change for the political expedient it was. They protested that it was based on principles unsuitable for a democracy, striking "at the very heart of the relationship of men in uniform to the society they served." They suspected—rightly, as it turned out—that the politicians would not provide the funds and incentives to make it work, and that it could become a haven for rejects. The other services feared that removal of the threat provided by the draft would cripple their recruiting. Top officers throughout the military predicted that the All-Volunteer Force would fail, further weakening American defenses and endangering the national security.[15]

Such fears seemed borne out in the first years of the experiment. The military tinkered with various incentives to make enlistment attractive—even discussing, before quickly discarding, the radical notion that officers might salute enlisted personnel to show they were there to serve them. It speeded the integration of women, a revolutionary step that became expedient as well as politically correct with the elimination of the draft. As predicted, the embattled Nixon and Carter administrations did not secure the funds to make the volunteer force work, and lingering anti-militarism made recruitment difficult. As late as 1979, what Chief of Staff Gen. Edward "Shy" Meyer called a "hollow army" was 15,000 short of its authorized strength, and the Air Force and Navy endured severe manpower problems. African Americans constituted a disproportionate percentage of the new Army, and critics warned that ghetto youths could be the cannon fodder of the next war. Experts continued to be troubled by the volunteer concept. "What kind of society excuses its most privileged members from defending it?" sociologist Charles Moskos pointedly asked. Recruits continued to be underqualified, and drug and alcohol problems persisted. By the end of the decade, there was much talk of restoring the draft.[16]

A second structural reform was largely the handiwork of Gen.

Creighton Abrams, Army Chief of Staff from 1972 to 1974. Like other senior officers, Abrams had been deeply frustrated by President Lyndon Baines Johnson's refusal to mobilize the reserves. As commander of U.S. forces in Vietnam from 1968 to 1972, he had had to deal with the results in terms of a depleted, unskilled, and demoralized army.

As Chief of Staff, Abrams set out to ensure this would not happen again. His essential task was to maintain the Army's fighting strength in the face of pressures to slash the military budget. To stave off further cuts, he made a deal with Secretary of Defense James Schlesinger—the so-called Golden Handshake—to build the Army from thirteen to sixteen divisions without increasing regular forces above 785,000. They did this through a revised force structure that assigned most support functions to the reserves, thus integrating reserves with regulars so closely that it would be impossible to disconnect them. Most significant, from Abrams's standpoint, regulars would not be able to function without the reserves, and thus a future commander in chief would not be able to do what LBJ had done in 1965. "They're not taking us to war again without calling up the reserves," Abrams remarked on numerous occasions.[17]

Abrams's initiative had a huge impact on future mobilizations. By the time of the Persian Gulf War, 70 percent of the Army's support services, 60 percent of the Air Force's strategic airlift units, and 93 percent of the Navy's cargo-handling battalions were with the reserves. A full 100 percent of the Military Traffic Management Command, which managed ports, air bases, and railyards, was with the reserves. President George Bush thus had no choice in 1990 but to call up the reserves and open a national debate on going to war. The subsequent peacekeeping operation in Bosnia also relied heavily on reserve units.[18]

The Vietnam debacle also provoked in the armed services what Col. Harry Summers has called a "renaissance" in military thought.[19] In the post–World War II era, a confident, even complacent American military establishment had all but ignored the study of war. Caught up in the organizational revolution of the 1950s, it focused on raising and managing its forces rather than on how to use them. Facing the uncertainties of a revolutionary new age of nuclear weapons, it left the field of strategic thought to civilian, largely academic theorists, who pioneered such voguish concepts as deterrence, limited war, escalation and coercion, and counter-insurgency.[20]

From the standpoint of Vietnam-era military officers, such theories had proven bankrupt in Vietnam, and in the aftermath they sought to regain control of their own bailiwick and get back to basics. Ironically, the revolution began in the Navy, traditionally the most conservative of the services. As president of the Naval War College, Vice Admiral Stansfield Turner in 1972 introduced into the curriculum a required course on strategy. The course drew heavily on history. To the consternation of some students enrolled in the initial classes, it went all the way back to Thucydides. Along with the focus on strategy came a rediscovery of the German military thinker Carl von Clausewitz, who had articulated the intimate and intricate connections between war and politics; and a shift of emphasis from the science to the art of war.[21]

The "Turner Revolution" swept the armed services in the 1970s. Courses on strategy were introduced at the Air War College and Army War College, and Clausewitz was the man of the hour. All the services rediscovered history and devoted substantial resources to the study of war. In 1979, the Army started a Combat Studies Institute at Fort Leavenworth that taught historically oriented courses in the Command and General Staff College and conducted research on issues related to doctrine. The Navy created a Strategic Studies Group in Newport.[22] Thus, while academia in general and the historical profession in particular suffered through a horrendous depression in the 1970s, history was a growth industry in the military.

In the wake of the Vietnam War and in light of the rediscovery of strategy, the services rewrote their "war-fighting" doctrines, an exercise that provoked often bitter debate about the lessons of Vietnam and how, if at all, they should be applied. Ironically, if not surprisingly, the greatest impact of the Vietnam experience was that it would have very little impact on the actual post-Vietnam doctrine, top officers in all the services generally agreeing that they would not fight that type of war again.

Conflict within the Navy set the tone for the larger debate. In light of the Korean and Vietnam experiences, Zumwalt tried to reconfigure his service for diverse missions. As the top U.S. naval officer in Vietnam, he had demonstrated ingenuity and adaptability in using his forces for the unique problems posed by the war. As CNO, he sought to rebuild the Navy to handle conventional war, limited war, and gunboat diplomacy by constructing what he called "low" ships (as opposed to heavy aircraft carriers) for a variety of different sea control missions. He was defeated by a coalition of powerful forces inside and outside the Navy representing enthusiasts for airpower and submarines. In the 1980s, under the aggressive leadership of secretary John Lehman, the Navy reverted to its traditional absorption with the Soviet threat and set out to build a 600-vessel fleet centered around aircraft carriers. To the post-Zumwalt Navy, Vietnam was irrelevant.[23]

The Army could not cast Vietnam aside so easily, of course, but its major doctrinal thrust was also in other directions. Senior officers recognized that the Army had not been well prepared for fighting in 1965, and after the war they established a Training and Doctrine Command (TRADOC) to better prepare soldiers for the next conflict, the first time that responsibility for research, training, and doctrine had been placed under a single command. Its first leader was Gen. William DePuy, one of Westmoreland's top assistants when he had headed the Military Assistance Command, Vietnam, and the architect of the much-maligned search-and-destroy strategy used in Vietnam from 1965 to 1968. Like other military leaders after Vietnam, DePuy naturally—and gladly—turned to the Soviet threat. The Yom Kippur War of 1973, rather than Vietnam, became the Army's model for the next war.[24]

The doctrine developed under DePuy's guidance focused on conventional warfare in Europe and, in the words of one commentator, "aimed to 'expunge' the bitter experience of Vietnam."[25] Conceding that in the anticipated conflict with Warsaw Pact armies on the plains of Central Europe NATO forces would likely be outnumbered, Field Manual 100–5 of 1976 outlined the new concept of Active Defense, a radical departure from the army's traditional offensive doctrine and piling-on approach, and placed great emphasis on winning the first battle.[26]

These new concepts provoked considerable opposition in the Army, and thus a modified AirLand doctrine, as it evolved in the 1980s, emphasized the coordination of airpower with armor, ground forces, artillery, and even special forces, and the use of new high-tech weaponry to provide the speed, maneuverability, and firepower to enable smaller forces to defeat a larger army. Surprise and mobility were the keys to success. In the spirit of Robert E. Lee and Stonewall Jackson, the new doctrine called for deep probes, 100 miles or so behind enemy front lines, to find and exploit weak spots.[27]

Postwar Army doctrine moved ever further from Vietnam. Advocates of counterinsurgency and what came to be called low-intensity conflict (LIC) waged a rearguard action against the new conventional wisdom. There was some discussion of the strategic lessons of Vietnam in the Army War College publication *Parameters,* and the 1986 edition of FM 100–5 gave some attention to low-intensity conflict. But another major Army publication, *Military Review,* showed little interest in Vietnam, and the 1986 field manual made only passing reference to it. The Army's semiofficial, neo-Clausewitzian analysis, Col. Summers's *On Strategy* (1981), even wrote insurgency out of that war, arguing that after 1965 the United States faced a conventional threat and should have fought it as such. "Vietnam is such a nasty word in the American vocabulary today," one officer observed in 1980, "that even military men are loath to look back on it for lessons applicable to the future."[28]

The most bitter struggle took place in the Air Force. The youngest of the services, the Air Force was not inclined toward self-criticism or disposed to look searchingly at the Vietnam experience. Discussion of that war in professional military journals during the 1970s was almost nonexistent. Insofar as the leadership dealt with Vietnam, it sought vindication of long-standing beliefs, conveniently concluding that airpower had won the war in 1972 only to have it lost by the politicians. A small group of "Young Turks" tried to challenge that position in the 1980s, examining the role of airpower critically and thoughtfully, but they met stubborn resistance. Some were not promoted. When the *Air University Review* became an organ for the dissidents, it was closed down, ostensibly because it was not read and to save money. Discussion of low-intensity conflict nevertheless persisted in Air Force circles, and a 1992 operational manual stood conventional airpower theory on its ear by emphasizing that because insurgents presented few targets, airpower could best be used in such conflicts to support internal security forces. Such heretical notions never penetrated the top leadership, however, and post–Gulf War doctrine reclaimed the old high ground, insisting that in the new era of the revolution in military affairs (RMA), airpower could be counted upon to play the decisive role by destroying an enemy's ability to control information. This narrow focus on "information dominance," critics warned, might deprive the Air Force of the capacity to deal with less sophisticated enemies, as in Vietnam. "The increased interplay of information systems in war will not negate the fact that war is an intrinsically human enterprise, subject to vagaries of chance, fog, and friction."[29]

The services put great emphasis on improved training in the aftermath of Vietnam—in particular, hands-on, realistic training and rigorous self-criticism. Here again the Navy was the first to act. Alarmed by the heavy losses of aircraft and pilots in missions over North Vietnam, it instituted its much-ballyhooed Top Gun program in 1969, a postgraduate course in dogfighting for young pilots. The idea was to recreate as closely as possible the actual combat conditions experienced in Vietnam. New pilots were thus sent up against planes similar to those of the enemy using tactics employed by the enemy. After each training exercise, students went through intensive analysis of what had happened and why. The realistic training paid off immediately in improved performance and lighter losses.[30] The Air Force followed suit with its Red Flag program at Nellis Air Base in Nevada and went further by creating a squadron of "aggressor" aircraft to replicate the enemy, putting pilots under stress comparable to that of actual combat.[31]

The Army opened its National Training Center in the Mojave Desert in 1981. NTC, another product of DePuy's tenure at TRADOC, was a more ambitious replication of Top Gun and Red Flag. A fanatic on training, DePuy established standards for everything from marksmanship to the number of push-ups required for individual soldiers. Like the Navy and Air Force, the Army shifted from static, firing-range-type training to "free-form, force on force tactical engagements." Units were sent to NTC for two weeks' daytime and nighttime training against forces dressed like Soviets, carrying Soviet weapons, and employing Soviet tactics. NTC sought to make the experience as real as possible through battle conditions and live fire. As with the Navy and Air Force, the new training involved a basic change in culture. Shedding the "arrogance of the perennial winner," the post-Vietnam Army deliberately put aside the "can-do" and "zero defects" mentality of the post–World War II years that allowed no room for mistakes in favor of self-criticism and honest assessment of error. "Learning through failure" was the byword for a new era.[32]

The Marine Corps was a special case. With a long tradition of fighting low-intensity wars in tropical areas, the Marines were certain that their pacification strategy could have worked in Vietnam if it had been applied on a broader scale, and they were less disposed than other services to reexamine their experience in that war. In the rethinking of mission and doctrine that characterized the post-Vietnam era, however, the Marines were also less clear about their role than at any point in the recent past, and there was even talk of eliminating them as a separate service. The truck-bombing of a Marine barracks in Beirut in 1983, which killed 249 Americans, left them "reeling."[33]

Under the direction of Secretary of the Navy James Webb, an ex-Marine, and Commandant Al Gray, the Marines went through their own renaissance in the late 1980s. Gray resolved a long-standing debate between advocates of attrition and advocates of maneuver by adapting to Marine doctrine the Army's "fluid, flexible" warfare designed to sweep around enemy strengths and seek out weaknesses. He upgraded Marine training by establishing realistic conditions as in the other services, adding a week of Basic Warrior Training to boot camp and requiring that every Marine, no matter the job, be a rifleman. "We're warriors, and people who support warriors," he proclaimed, "and we must always keep that focus."[34]

Reorganization of the command system—perhaps the most fundamental reform of the post-Vietnam years—was imposed by Congress in 1986 over the opposition of the Joint Chiefs of Staff (JCS) and much of the Pentagon. It stemmed directly from the abysmal lack of coordination among the services that marred the invasion of Grenada in 1983, but in a much deeper sense it reflected perceived "lessons" of Vietnam. Throughout the Vietnam War, the Joint Chiefs had chafed at their lack of a formal position within the chain of command and their lack of influence with the civilian leadership. Under the JCS system at that time, the chiefs were more representatives of the individual services than independent military advisers to the president, which often resulted in watered-down recommendations that reflected the least common denominator of what they could agree upon. Bitter wrangling between the services in Washington and in the field hampered planning and crippled performance. An incredibly convoluted command system placed the Commander-in-Chief, Pacific (CINCPAC), a naval officer in Pearl

Harbor, over the entire operation and deprived the field commander, Gen. Westmoreland, of control of air operations over North Vietnam.[35]

The Goldwater-Nichols Defense Reorganization Act of 1986, labeled by one authority the "most sweeping military reform legislation in the history of the nation," sought to address these problems.[36] The position of Chairman, Joint Chiefs of Staff, was enhanced by making that individual the principal military adviser to the president and the Secretary of Defense, giving him responsibility for devising strategic plans and budgets, and assigning him a seat on the National Security Council. To improve cooperation among the services, the legislation placed great emphasis on "jointness." The Joint Staff, an advisory body that had previously served the chiefs as a group, was placed directly under the chairman, increased in size, and given greater responsibility. Training for joint service was made mandatory for senior officers, and joint courses were added to the curriculum at the various service schools. Field commanders were given greater authority over the forces under them. The legislation sought nothing less than a "complete organizational revolution."[37]

III

Within ten years after the fall of Saigon, a full-scale military resurgence was under way. Upon taking office in 1981, the administration of Ronald Reagan committed itself to wage the Cold War vigorously and poured billions of dollars into a massive military buildup. Popular attitudes shifted dramatically, most notably in a reawakening of patriotism and a respect for things military. The reforms initiated by the services in the wake of Vietnam began to show dramatic results. "2.1 million uniformed men and women are at home with the nation they serve," *U.S. News & World Report* exulted in 1985, "enjoying an esteem unimaginable a few years ago."[38] Signs of the military rebirth were everywhere. Moribund in 1979, the All-Volunteer Force was alive and well by the mid-1980s, a result of the Army's slick "Be All That You Can Be" advertising campaign and the pay increases and other incentives provided by the Reagan defense budgets.[39] The payoff was evident in more and better recruits, higher rates of reenlistment, and a better-trained and more proficient Army. As the Army went, so also the other services. The service academies were flooded with applications. Once kicked off numerous college campuses, ROTC (Reserve Officers' Training Corps) recovered and in some areas flourished. Popular support for the military grew dramatically. "Today, there's no fear that somebody's going to run up to you and give you hell about being in the army," a retired colonel said with obvious relief.[40] "The United States has shed its post-Vietnam doldrums of doubt, despair, and dissolution," boasted Assistant Secretary of Defense Richard Armitage.[41]

Even though the military had rebuilt itself by the mid-1980s, fears of another Vietnam still haunted its leaders. Indeed, nowhere in American society was there greater reluctance to employ force than in the military itself, a clear result of what had come to be called the "Vietnam syndrome." Senior military officers were "seared by the experience of public repudiation by large segments of society."[42] They brought from Vietnam a keen sense of the limits of public tolerance for a protracted war and a profound distrust of civilian leaders, who, many believed, poorly understood the uses of military power and were responsive to all sorts of political pressures that had little to do with the "objective conditions of the battlefield." "Remember one lesson from the Vietnam era," Gen. William Knowlton told Army War College graduates in 1985. "Those who ordered the meal were not there when the waiter brought the check."[43] Many officers also brought from Vietnam a new awareness of the limits of military power in resolving complex political problems such as insurgencies and civil conflicts. "We've thrown over the old 'can-do' idea," a senior officer told *New York Times* military correspondent Drew Middleton. "Now we want to know exactly what they want us to do and how they think it can be accomplished."[44]

This new attitude was palpable in the 1980s even as America's military machine was being rebuilt. Senior officers vigorously opposed the application of "small doses of force in messy waters for obscure political purposes." They opposed committing troops to vaguely defined missions such as the 1983 peacekeeping operation in Lebanon. They opposed sending anything more than small advisory units to the raging civil conflicts in Central America, and worried that even these small commitments might put the United States on a slippery slope toward full-scale intervention as in Vietnam.[45]

The military's post-Vietnam fears were articulated in late 1984 by Secretary of Defense Caspar Weinberger. The so-called Weinberger doctrine was an immediate reaction to the 1983 bombing of the Marine barracks in Lebanon and also to the persistent advocacy by Secretary of State George Shultz and Reagan's National Security Council of committing small increments of forces to what Weinberger dismissed as "ever more wild adventures."[46] But the secretary later conceded that his views had been primarily shaped by the "terrible mistake" of committing troops in Vietnam without ensuring popular support and providing them the means to win. In the summer of 1984, Weinberger thus framed a set of rules for "the uses of military power." Troops would be committed only as a last resort and only if it was plainly in the national interest. Objectives must be clearly defined and attainable. Public support must be assured, and the means provided to ensure victory.[47]

Weinberger's initiative provoked a "bloody fight" within the Reagan administration. Critical journalists dismissed his rules as "the Capgun Doctrine" and the "doctrine of only-fun-wars"; Shultz later labeled them the "Vietnam syndrome in spades."[48] The "doctrine" was never given official sanction, but top military officers such as future Joint Chiefs chairman Colin Powell, while conceding the dangers of stating such rules publicly and explicitly, accepted them in principle. "Clausewitz would have applauded," Powell later wrote. "And in the future when it became my responsibility to advise presidents on committing our forces to combat, Weinberger's rules turned out to be a practical guide." They became the rules under which the Persian Gulf War was fought.[49]

IV

Indeed, in many ways, the Persian Gulf War at times seemed for the military (and for the rest of American society) more about Vietnam than about Kuwait, oil, and Iraq. Those officers and noncoms who had experienced the agony of Vietnam saw the Gulf War as an opportunity for redemption. Much like an athlete preparing for a championship match, they felt special pressures as they awaited battle. "Years later, going into Desert Storm," a senior naval officer recalled, "the common theme among all leaders who had been involved in Vietnam was, 'We want to do this one right.'" An Air Force Chief Warrant Officer agreed: "I kept thinking Vietnam. . . . This time we're going to prove we can really win."[50]

From beginning to end, in every conceivable way, the military and the civilian leadership consciously set out to avoid the mistakes they believed had been made in Vietnam. As a result of the Abrams reforms, the reserves had to be mobilized at the outset of the crisis, binding the nation to the war in a way it had not been bound in Vietnam. Following the Weinberger "rules" to the letter, President George Bush carefully cultivated public support and secured a vote of endorsement from Congress before launching military action against Iraq.

In method and result, military planning was distinctly different from that in the Vietnam War. Although the civilian leadership had to push the military relentlessly to launch the ground offensive, Bush was generally content to leave military planning in the hands of the field commander, and he went to great lengths to avoid the appearance of micromanagement from Washington that had become identified with Lyndon Johnson. He repeatedly insisted that "this would not be another Vietnam." American troops would not fight with one hand tied behind their back. There would be no gradualism or conceded sanctuary. "Once you're committed to war," Gen. H. Norman Schwarzkopf observed, "be ferocious enough to do whatever is necessary to get it over with as quickly as possible."[51] Even the original name assigned to the air campaign—INSTANT THUNDER—highlighted the differences from its discredited Vietnam-era predecessor. In contrast to Vietnam, where an overconfident military had initially dismissed the enemy, the Iraqi army was portrayed as ten feet tall, although knowledgeable officials knew better. Gens. Powell and Schwarzkopf refused to be pushed into war until they had massed absolutely overwhelming force to apply against the enemy.

The command system worked differently. Schwarzkopf and his commanders carefully avoided what they saw as the mistakes of Vietnam: "giving cavalier promises and 'sugarcoating the truth' . . . to please the commander in chief."[52] Rather than do this, officers were prepared to contemplate resignation, something they had concluded their predecessors should have done in Vietnam. As a result of Goldwater-Nichols, Schwarzkopf had much greater control of the forces in the Gulf than Westmoreland had had in Vietnam. His commanders had to listen to him rather than to their respective services.[53]

Certain that a hostile media had contributed to failure in Vietnam and concluding that war was too important to be left to the journalists, the military, with the cooperation of civilian authorities, muzzled the press. Access to the battlefield was strictly limited. All dispatches had to be submitted to military censors in Washington and in the field. To hide from the public the cost of the war, the military even restricted coverage of the return to the United States of the bodies of those killed in action. "It's okay to die for your country," the columnist James McCartney acidly observed. "The Pentagon just doesn't want anyone to know about it."[54]

The nation's smashing and stunningly easy victory in the Persian Gulf War seemed for many Americans—military and civilian—a long-awaited vindication. "After the ambiguity and humiliation of Vietnam," observed Gerald Linderman of the University of Michigan, "the gulf war seems a model of clarity and success, a war portrayed as being fought with the most efficient weapons and greatest resolve against the vilest of villains."[55] "We've closed the door on Vietnam," one officer proclaimed. "We've done it. The circle is complete."[56]

V

The Gulf War in fact helped erase bad memories of Vietnam for the military and for civilians and restored the prestige and self-respect of the armed forces. The performance of the U.S. military in the Gulf War seemed to vindicate the reforms instituted in the 1970s and 1980s. Many writers have thus concluded that the services learned from their earlier failure and that their constructive response to the Vietnam debacle was the key to rebuilding an efficient, devastatingly effective modern war-making machine and to success in the Gulf.[57]

The legacy of America's longest and most divisive war is far more complex and far-reaching than that, however. A deep residue of suspicion about civilian leadership still lingers from Vietnam. It has, together with the end of the Cold War and the removal of the Soviet threat, the emergence of a strange new world of peacekeeping missions in distant areas, and fundamental changes in the way forces are raised and used, created a widening gap between the military and society that has possibly huge implications for U.S. foreign policy and civil-military relations in the twenty-first century.

The Gulf War's apparent vindication of post-Vietnam military doctrine, for example, could turn out to be counterproductive. That war, to reverse Gen. Omar Bradley's famous statement about expanding the Korean War, was the right war in the right place at the right time against the right enemy. It was the perfect war for forces trained to do battle with the Soviets on the plains of eastern Europe; the desert was the perfect killing field for the military's new doctrines of mobile warfare.

The Gulf War thus powerfully reinforced the military's post-Vietnam focus on conventional, high-tech war. Current Air Force doctrine is entirely conventional. The Army is now experiencing something of an identity crisis, unsure whether to remake itself into a peacekeeping force or continue to focus on conventional warfare, twenty-first-century style. Its most recent manual has a chapter titled "Operations Other than War," but still heavily emphasizes high-tech, mobile war in the mode of Desert Storm. Outside of the Marine Corps, with its tradition of fighting small wars and its current boast to be the nation's "911 force," the services are left with a "structure, doctrine and attitude that are still not conducive to involvement in low intensity conflict."[58] Despite all the recent hype about a revolution in military affairs, this type of war may be the most likely contingency in a new and as yet quite uncertain era. The military may thus find itself—in part as a result of its abiding determination to avoid anything resembling Vietnam—unprepared for or irrelevant to the challenges of the twenty-first century.

Prevailing notions about the role of the press in wartime, also deeply influenced by the Vietnam experience, must be addressed as well. In light of recent trends in journalism, few would argue for unlimited press coverage of combat operations, and the technology of modern journalism will create far more difficult problems for the military in future wars. This said, the notion that the press lost the war in Vietnam remains, especially among military people, one of the most persistent and pernicious of the many myths of that war. The sort of censorship that was applied in the Gulf War—a legacy of Vietnam—probably could not have survived the pressures of a protracted war. Some means must be found in future wars to reconcile the legitimate concerns of national security with the public's need and right to know.[59]

The Goldwater-Nichols reforms produced an improved command system for the Gulf War and at least slightly improved cooperation among the services, but they may also have helped bring to the surface a long-simmering "hidden crisis" in civil-military relations and raised at least a potential threat to civilian control of the military. In a provocative and highly controversial article published in 1994, historian Richard Kohn warned that Gen. Colin Powell had taken advantage of Goldwater-Nichols, the force of his own personality, and the weakness of the civilian leadership to become "the most formidable military figure in this country in two generations." And he used that power in ways that Kohn found disturbing. It was Powell, not his civilian superiors, who devised the military force structure for the post–Cold War era, and Powell whose role in the Gulf War far exceeded even that envisioned for the post-reform Chairman, JCS. When the Clinton administration in its early days proposed easing the ban against homosexuals' serving in the military, Powell and the JCS undermined the proposals rather than implement them, thus, in effect, usurping choices that should have been made by civilians.[60]

Critics have further warned that the often decisive role played by the military in recent years in determining when, where, and how troops would be used abroad endangers the principle of civilian control. Among top military leaders, the Vietnam syndrome persisted past the Gulf War, and the Weinberger doctrine continued to provide their operating principles. In Vietnam, Powell has written, "the top leadership never went to the secretary of defense or the president and said, 'This war is unwinnable the way we are fighting it.' Many of my generation . . . vowed that when our time came to call the shots we would not quietly acquiesce in half-hearted warfare for half-baked reasons that the American people could not understand or support."[61]

In the 1990s, military leaders steadfastly opposed commitment of forces in such places as Haiti and the former Yugoslavia, in effect rejecting missions that did not suit their preferences and priorities.

In 1992, Powell *publicly* opposed U.S. intervention in war-torn Bosnia because, he said, a decisive victory was not attainable. Claiming that the military had learned the "proper lessons of history," an obvious allusion to Vietnam and a claim to superior wisdom that he and his colleagues did not, in fact, possess, he went on to pronounce that "as soon as they tell me it is limited, it means they do not care whether you achieve a result or not. As soon as they tell me 'surgical,' I head for the bushes." By acting in this fashion, historian Russell Weigley has warned, Powell overstepped his bounds, blatantly intruding in the political process and advancing a political position that was not properly his to take.[62]

When the United States did commit troops to Bosnia in 1995, a military still obsessed with "mission security" and avoidance of casualties dictated the terms. The military's paranoia about a "fuzzy mission" led to rules of engagement that sharply restricted the use of American forces, preventing them from pursuing war criminals or assisting the relocation of refugees and thus limiting their ability to implement the Dayton Accords. Their insistence on an "exit strategy" led to the imposition of an unrealistic (and later scrapped) twelve-month deadline for the removal of U.S. troops. Whether the military leaders' concerns about the dangers of intervention are right or wrong is not the issue here. In fact, in both Haiti and Bosnia, they appear to have grossly overestimated the potential casualties. The point is, rather, that they have increasingly dictated for their own reasons decisions that should properly be made by civilians on the basis of political considerations. Critics such as Kohn and Weigley thus see a dangerous reversal of the old Clausewitzian dictum, warning that political decisions are being made on essentially military grounds.[63] The increasing difficulty of getting a semiautonomous military to do civilian bidding is, in the eyes of some defense experts, at least "worrisome."[64]

In the Gulf War, the All-Volunteer Force and the Abrams reforms—perhaps the most important legacies of Vietnam—seem to have proven their value. Defense analyst Jeffrey Record has speculated, however, that had the Gulf War lasted longer than a year and the rotation of large numbers of troops been required, the United States might not have been able to replace its frontline troops with a skilled force adequate to sustain a long war. Record has further observed that the questionable performance of some ill-prepared National Guard and reserve units points up basic weaknesses in the system that, if not corrected, could cause major problems in a longer war with a competitive foe. The Abrams reforms have hamstrung mobilization for the Bosnia operation. As that mission extended far beyond the original deadline and Army officials were compelled to call up more and more reservists, they began to wonder how long civilians would put up with being taken away from families and careers for hazardous, low-paying jobs in remote countries.[65]

In the post–Cold War era, the future of the volunteer system appears at best murky. No doubt it was one of the success stories of the 1980s. It seems evident that volunteers perform better than draftees, and raising troops through a volunteer system may be more equitable than the post–World War II draft. Reinstitution of the draft might also deny minorities opportunities they have had under the existing system, and forcing people to serve against their will damages cohesion. In any event, return of the draft in any foreseeable circumstance is doubtful. It remains to be seen, however, whether volunteer forces can be recruited and sustained at a high level of proficiency in an era with a robust civilian economy, when the military's mission seems increasingly unclear and when downsizing and budget-cutting may eliminate or reduce some of the incentives. Long hours in training and frequent tours of duty abroad have also taken their toll. The number of young males enlisting has declined since 1989. The Army failed to meet its recruitment quotas in 1997, and the Navy in early 1999 faced a shortfall of 7,000 recruits and had 22,000 empty billets in the fleet. Both the Navy and Air Force have had great difficulty recruiting pilots. For the first time in years, there was talk of a possible return to the draft and, more likely, a lowering of standards for recruits.[66]

As critics have pointed out from the beginning, a volunteer military force poses even more fundamental problems in terms of the place of the military in American society. In what turned out to be her farewell speech (she was forced to resign for allegedly derogatory remarks about the Marines in the same speech), former Assistant Secretary of the Army Sara Lister warned in late 1997 of a "widening cultural gap between our armed services and the rest of us." As a result of the volunteer system and the end of the Cold War, most Americans no longer serve in the armed forces or even know people in the military. They are largely indifferent to things military. With few exceptions, the civilians now making decisions have no military background. Who has more military experience than Bill Clinton, Newt Gingrich, and Phil Gramm combined? goes a recent joke that sounds suspiciously of military origin. The answer is Shannon Faulkner, the woman who spent several well-publicized days at The Citadel in 1996 before dropping out.[67]

The military, on the other hand, increasingly stands apart from society as a whole. Without the draft, few upper- or upper-middle-class Americans now serve in the armed forces, and college graduates in enlisted ranks are rare. A growing demand for technological skills has also led the military to shut its doors to those from poor backgrounds. The armed services thus now include neither elites nor the poor, and they are less representative of society at large. They have become increasingly professionalized. They are also politically more conservative today than in the recent past, and they have become more partisan and more openly politicized. One survey suggests that two-thirds of the officer corps voted Republican in 1996, compared to less than one-third in 1976. Isolated on ships or on remote bases, mostly in the West and South and away from metropolitan coastal elites, members of the military live by a set of shared values and operate according to a code of beliefs and behavior different from that of their civilian counterparts. They view themselves as standing above the selfish, fragmented, and undisciplined civilian society they are pledged to defend and for which many have a certain contempt. Journalist Thomas Ricks has recently described the Marine Corps as a "military subculture within a military subculture that is becoming increasingly disdainful of civilian society."[68]

This widening gap has unsettling, if as yet unclear, implications. Civilian leaders have at best a poor understanding of military concerns and military issues. As part of its "Vietnam hangover," on the other hand, the military retains deep-seated suspicions about a civilian leadership that allegedly betrayed it before and might do so again, suspicions that are being passed down to the post-Vietnam generation. "The U.S. military is now more alienated from its civilian leadership than at any time in American history, and more vocal about it," Kohn warned in 1994. "The next war we fight is likely to be on American soil," writers in the *Marine Gazette* predicted, referring to a war against the chaos that characterizes the society at large. Kohn contends that the danger of a coup is "virtually nil" and that the problems in civil-military relations will probably work themselves out, as in the past. But he and others suggest that, at a minimum, active steps should be taken to restore civilian control, rebuild the diversity of the officer corps, and promote greater trust and mutual respect between civilians and the military.[69]

The legacy of Vietnam for the military has thus been enormous. The immediate impact was devastating: the destruction and demoralization of a once-proud and seemingly invincible machine. Precisely because of this, the military in some ways faced up to a war most Americans preferred to sweep under the rug, healing itself, enthusiastically and energetically embracing *institutional* changes that transformed its basic culture, and putting together a high-tech machine that performed with deadly efficiency in the Persian Gulf War.

This represents only a part of the story, however. While adapting its institutions, the military has been less successful in adjusting intellectually and emotionally to the trauma of Vietnam. There has been a marked reluctance on its part to accept a share of responsibility for the nation's failure. The tendency, rather, has been to blame a weak-kneed civilian leadership or a lack of public will. The Museum of Military History at the Marine base at Parris Island, South Carolina, for example, teaches that "American forces, though never defeated in battle, were removed from war by a wavering government and a divided populace"—a conviction, Thomas Ricks adds, that is "gospel throughout the Corps."[70] Such views have made it difficult for all the services to reevaluate their strategy and tactics in Vietnam, to analyze the peculiar demands of low-intensity conflict, and to develop doctrines appropriate for what could be the dominant form of conflict in the twenty-first century. The legacy of deep suspicion bequeathed by Vietnam has left the military reluctant to employ forces abroad except under the most favorable circumstances and has pushed its top officers to intrude into the political decision-making process in ways in which they have not done before. Such suspicion has contributed, along with other changes resulting from Vietnam, to a widening gap between the military and society that has possibly serious implications for the future. The impact of Vietnam thus has persisted well beyond the Persian Gulf War, and may last long beyond the careers of the people who fought in Southeast Asia.

Revolutionary Heroism and Politics in Postwar Vietnam

■

ROBERT K. BRIGHAM

Growing up in the 1960s in a working-class town in New York, as I did, meant friends and relatives went off to Vietnam with regularity. Many did not come back. Sadly, the sorrow of war touched my family, as it did thousands of American and Vietnamese families. From an early age, I was obsessed with the war. The television war occupied much of my time, perhaps too much time. Eventually, this personal obsession turned into an academic interest, and I found myself majoring in history in college.

I focused my undergraduate studies on the history of American foreign relations. After earning a master's degree in the same field, I team-taught courses on the war with a Vietnamese refugee from Saigon. He tutored me in Vietnamese and encouraged me to travel to his country to learn more about the conflict. In 1989, I joined a group of American academics who traveled throughout Vietnam, Laos, and Cambodia meeting with scholars and government officials. This experience had a profound impact on my teaching and scholarship and persuaded me to pursue a Ph.D. with George Herring at the University of Kentucky.

During my studies in Lexington, I took formal Vietnamese-language classes at Cornell University and traveled to Vietnam for research on several occasions. I was one of the first American scholars given access to the Vietnamese archives on the war, and I wrote my dissertation on the National Liberation Front's foreign policy.

After earning my Ph.D. in 1994, I joined the History Department at Vassar College. Since then, I have traveled to Vietnam regularly for research and have published widely in Vietnamese and English. A particular joy for me now is taking my students to Vietnam. Several Vietnamese Americans have joined me on these trips, visiting their families for the first time in nearly twenty years. Veterans and Gold Star Mothers have come with me on other journeys, as we all try to come to terms with the tragedy of Vietnam.

■

The Vietnam War has had a dramatic impact on Vietnamese political culture and institutions. In 1960, at its Third National Congress, the Vietnamese Communist Party (VCP) promoted the principle of collective leadership to avoid a damaging power struggle after President Ho Chi Minh's inevitable death. Party leaders correctly predicted that a conflict over succession would threaten the modern revolution and frustrate their war effort against the United States and its Saigon ally. This first generation of leaders believed that no individual should gain predominant power and that the cult of solidarity promised political stability and longevity for their cause. Those Party officials selected for high office in 1960 remained in their posts throughout the war. In the postwar period, Vietnam's Communist officials have continued to rely on collective leadership and shared power to retain their control over the political process. Two generations of Political Bureau leaders have been replaced, yet the Party continues to enjoy a monopoly on political power.

This essay, utilizing the latest Vietnamese-language sources available, examines the impact of the Vietnam War on postwar political life. It suggests that the Communist Party has maintained political control in Vietnam partly by cultivating the image of collective revolutionary heroism. It also argues that postwar institutional reform has narrowed the political process within the Party and, as a result, the first stirrings of ideological pluralism have emerged. Critics outside the regime have surfaced as well, threatening the Party's exclusive ownership of national sacrifice as it relates to political legitimacy.

As the Party faced internal and external pressure to reform in the late 1980s and early 1990s, it relied more heavily upon the concept of revolutionary heroism to maintain its advantage in Hanoi. By *revolutionary heroism,* I refer to the promotion of the Party as the vanguard of the struggle against foreign invaders through the purposeful manipulation of images of sacrifice for the fatherland. Like many of its neighbors, Vietnam has a paternalistic political culture that makes promotion of the revolutionary hero a common and almost necessary component of political life. The concept of the collective hero, with roots in Vietnam's Buddhist and Confucian past, supports a hierarchical view of social relationships and stresses social order. Professor Nguyen Khac Vien of Hanoi University writes, "Bourgeois individualism, which puts personal interests ahead of those of society[,] and petty bourgeois anarchism, which allows no social discipline whatsoever, are alien to both Confucianism and Marxism."[1] One of the great successes of the revolution was its ability to tie Vietnam's past to its future.

Within this framework, the Party created national heroes out of those who sacrificed for the revolution. Celebration of this sacrifice gave the Party preponderant power to assemble a pantheon of champions, such as Ho Chi Minh and Vo Nguyen Giap, tied to Vietnam's glorious past. Throughout the war, Party publications stressed revolutionary continuity and national sacrifice.[2] According to historian William Duiker, the VCP had used the personality of Ho Chi Minh to "cement the Party's reputation as the legitimate representative of Vietnamese national tradition as well as the leading force in the Vietnamese revolution."[3] One experienced American reporter told fellow journalist Frances FitzGerald during the war that he finally realized the United States would never win "when I noticed that all of the street signs in Saigon were named after Vietnamese heroes who fought against foreign invaders."[4]

In the postwar period, the Party promoted its collective revolutionary elite as keepers of the flame with direct ties to Ho Chi Minh, the Trung sisters, Le Loi, and Nguyen Hue.[5] Party leaders stressed continuity in the sacrifice for national salvation of the fatherland and even rewarded individual families for such efforts. In 1994, the Party issued an ordinance conferring the title of "Hero Mother of Vietnam" on those mothers whose only son or whose only two children "laid down their lives for the national cause."[6] Hanoi hoped such actions would galvanize popular support for its postwar program.

The transition from war to peace was difficult, however, and the Party soon depended even more upon its leading revolutionary role as its primary claim to political legitimacy. Prime Minister Pham Van Dong understood the problem in the early 1980s all too well: "Yes, we defeated the United States. But now we are plagued by problems. We do not have enough to eat. We are a poor, underdeveloped nation. Waging war is simple, but running a country is very difficult."[7]

The prime minister's remarks reflect Vietnam's economic and political difficulties in the postwar period. Economic troubles began shortly after the military victory in April 1975. The Party had assured non-Communists living in the south that their "property and profits were secure."[8] In March 1978, however, in sharp contrast to its rhetoric, the Party nationalized all business and commercial activity above the family level and constructed agricultural collectives. The result was an unmitigated economic disaster. Inflation was rampant, and there were severe shortages in basic foodstuffs, such as rice and tea. Hundreds of thousands of people fled the country as the government continued to pursue its failed economic policies into the early 1980s. The Party's political difficulties also emerged soon after the fall of Saigon.

In the immediate postwar period, the VCP faced a serious dilemma. Throughout the war, the Party had claimed that reunification of the country would take years, perhaps decades, resulting ultimately from negotiations between northerners and southerners. In the face of increasing domestic and international pressures, however, the Party moved swiftly toward reunification.[9] On November 15, 1975, representatives from the north and south met in Saigon for the Consultative Conference on National Reunification.[10] In just six days, Communist officials settled all issues of reunification. In a brief communiqué released shortly after the conference, Party leaders concluded:

> The conference was unanimous; on the method of unification of the country . . . a general election over the entire territory of Vietnam must be held soon to elect a common National Assembly. This National Assembly . . . will determine the structure of the state, elect the leading organs of the state, and prescribe the new constitution of a unified Vietnam.[11]

The editor of *Nhan Dan* (The People), the Party's daily newspaper, was quick to point out, however, that "the elections . . . to be held on April 25, 1976 . . . were not to decide the nature of the regime . . . that has been decided during the struggle."[12]

Indeed, since the Party's Third Congress in September 1960, the VCP's leading political institutions and personalities had remained the same, and Hanoi had no intention of changing either in the postwar period. "We had led the people in our struggle for national salvation," former foreign minister Nguyen Co Thach recently reported, "and we were the best prepared to move the nation in the proper direction. Beginning with the Third National Congress in 1960, we had developed the proper balance in political, diplomatic, and military affairs."[13] Most Party leaders do see the Third Congress as the turning point in the modern revolution.

When the Party gathered for its Third Congress in 1960, it had experienced five years of political turmoil. The VCP had ousted its secretary-general, Truong Chinh, for the failed land-reform campaign of 1954–56, and, as a result, president Ho Chi Minh had to assume full leadership responsibilities in the Party. Ho believed this was a dangerous practice and reportedly told a close friend, "I will not live forever, and I fear that the revolution is not prepared for my death."[14] Accordingly, the Third National Congress, under Ho's direction, adopted a collective-leadership strategy, ensuring that no single Party member would gain predominant power. It also established a bureaucratic structure that assured orderly succession. Specifically, the Party endorsed resolutions stating that no individual could simultaneously hold the positions of Party secretary-general and prime minister. The Congress solidified the role of the Political Bureau and, as a counterweight, strengthened the power of the Council of Ministers. It also enhanced the role of the Military Commission of the Political Bureau, ensuring political oversight of the army. The Party ultimately concluded that it "must correctly apply the system of collective leadership, combined with the division of responsibility, and the principles of Party life."[15]

These measures eventually limited political participation within the Party, making entrance to the highest policymaking institutions dependent on a shared strategic culture based on uniform historical experience. With respect to the concept of shared strategic culture, scholars usually refer to "grand strategic preferences" derived from a set of assumptions "about the nature of the conflict and the enemy."[16] These sets of assumptions are rooted deeply in shared historical experiences of the individuals and promote unity in strategic thinking.

Beginning with the Third National Congress and long into the post–Vietnam War period, no Party leader came to power who had not served the revolution in the First and Second Indochina Wars (1946–54 and 1956–75, respectively). All Political Bureau members were founders of the Indochinese Communist Party (1929), and all joined the Central Committee at the First National Congress in 1945. Most Central Committee members joined the Party during the 1940s and participated in the August Revolution in 1945.

Party leaders had other common historical experiences. Most revolutionaries had spent time in jail for their anticolonial activities.

"Almost everyone served time in French prisons," one Political Bureau member recalled. "It was a shared suffering that influenced our thinking."[17] Much of the political elite had also lost family members during the long struggle against the French. A Central Committee member commented recently, "Everyone I knew in Hanoi had lost loved ones. It left an indelible mark on our hearts and in our minds."[18] According to several Party leaders, this shared experience was the cornerstone of political life in Hanoi. "We had known each other for years," one Party leader explained, "and each of us knew what the others were thinking. You must remember, we all had the same experience and outlook on life."[19] Former Political Bureau member Nguyen Co Thach commented in a 1995 interview that "there were disagreements within the Political Bureau on occasion," but it was "easy to reach agreement quickly."[20] Political consensus was also assured because the Political Bureau approved membership to the Central Committee, and, in turn, the Central Committee ultimately selected the Political Bureau.

As the Party prepared for its Fourth National Congress in December 1976, its first postwar congress, few VCP leaders expected a political change. "We had led the country to freedom and independence," one Party leader said in 1996, "and now we were going to lead the country in peace."[21] Although each congress did replace nearly one-third of the Central Committee, these positions were held largely by individuals who had withdrawn or become inactive. "The Central Committee changed only through natural attrition," Prime Minister Pham Van Dong explained, "and replacements came from our revolutionary ranks."[22]

Indeed, the Central Committee did experience a generational change in some of its membership between the Third Congress in 1960 and the Fourth Congress in 1976, but there was an orderly succession. The VCP replaced aging revolutionaries with a younger generation of Party leaders who had similar backgrounds. Most new Central Committee members had joined the Party during the First Indochina War (against the French), and all had experience in the Second Indochina War (against the Americans). "There may have been a difference in age," one former Central Committee member recently reported, "but there was no difference in revolutionary legitimacy."[23] Continuity, therefore, characterized the Central Committee at the Fourth National Congress.

The Political Bureau, on the other hand, did experience one important change at the Fourth Congress. The Party dismissed long-time member Hoang Van Hoan from the VCP altogether. Hoan had been a strong supporter of Communist China throughout Vietnam's modern revolution, and Hanoi was growing increasingly estranged from its powerful neighbor. Hoan's dismissal was a signal to others that the Party would not tolerate any deviation from the approved path.

If there was a change in the Political Bureau's thinking between the Third Congress in 1960 and the Fourth Congress in 1976, it did concern its relationship with the Communist superpowers. Hanoi had long enjoyed good relations with Moscow and Beijing, but the growing Sino-Soviet dispute threatened to destroy the socialist alliance. During the war, the VCP had managed to chart a middle course, avoiding a major confrontation with either of its useful allies. By 1976, however, relations with Communist China had badly deteriorated, and VCP leaders adopted a policy more congenial to the Soviet Union. Critics of this decision were let go at the Fourth Congress, although membership in the Political Bureau remained relatively constant. Between 1960 and 1976, it lost only three members: President Ho Chi Minh and Nguyen Chi Thanh, head of the southern directorate (known in the West as COSVN), both died in office, and the Party dismissed Hoang Van Hoan.

Other important changes were announced at the Fourth National Congress. The VCP dismantled much of its wartime political structure, integrating the southern National Liberation Front (NLF) into the National United Front. The Party quickly replaced COSVN with a unified VCP command. Southern Communist mass associations, such as the Youth League, the Federation of Trade

Unions, and the Women's Union, also merged with their northern counterparts. In a now-famous scene on the parade platform in Saigon during the victory rally of May 15, 1975, former NLF member Truong Nhu Tang asked People's Army of Vietnam (PAVN) Senior General Van Tien Dung, "Where are the famous divisions of the National Liberation Front?" Dung replied coldly, "The army has already been unified."[24] By the time of the Fourth National Congress, therefore, the VCP had solidified its control over political life, dismissing any notion of alternative governmental structures or leaders.

Vietnam's postwar political problems did not end at the Fourth Congress, however. As the decade closed, the VCP found itself under attack on a number of fronts. In 1978, Pol Pot of Cambodia, the mastermind behind the Communist Khmer Rouge's "killing fields," ordered his followers to invade southern Vietnam to reclaim territory that had belonged to the Khmer peoples centuries before. Hanoi retaliated later that year, installing a friendly government in Phnom Penh and beginning a ten-year occupation of Cambodia. Most foreign leaders, even some friendly ones, condemned the VCP's aggressive action. The United States used Hanoi's retaliatory strikes to extend its postwar embargo against Vietnam.

In addition, the VCP found critics in every corner of Vietnam because of widely reported charges of corruption leveled at high-ranking officials. Severe rice shortages emerged in several provinces, as did a patronage system that would have made the bosses of Tammany Hall blush. Charges of corruption even circled around the heads of government in Hanoi, as some used their positions for personal gain.

To quiet domestic and international critics, Vietnam's National Assembly ratified a new constitution in 1980 that focused on corruption, foreign policy, and the economy. This document reflected the Party's belief that power was getting too concentrated within the Political Bureau and that a drastic change was necessary. Accordingly, the new constitution created a Council of State, headed by former secretary-general Truong Chinh. The Council was similar in composition and disposition to the Soviets' Presidium, with one important difference. In Moscow, Leonid Brezhnev served as both Party secretary and director of the Presidium. Vietnam's constitution ensured that this level of authority would never be given to one individual by making it impossible to hold the posts of secretary-general and chief of the Council of State simultaneously. The VCP purposefully selected Truong Chinh as a counterbalance to Secretary-General Le Duan, his longtime rival. "The Party always believed in consensus," one former VCP official recently stated, "but we always had counterweights at the highest levels of government."[25] Another Party leader declared, "The Council of State was a deliberate check on the growing power of the Political Bureau. Also, the complexities of life in postwar Vietnam demanded this new body."[26] The new constitution institutionalized the VCP's commitment to shared power, but it also paved the way for dramatic changes within the Party.

In March 1982, at the VCP's Fifth Congress, Party leaders worked closely with the Council of State, making a conscious effort to address pressing problems with "a new look at the top."[27] Several high-ranking VCP officials lost their prestigious posts, including Defense Minister General Vo Nguyen Giap, Minister of Economics Le Thanh Nghi, Foreign Minister Nguyen Duy Trinh, and Minister of the Interior Tran Quoc Hoan.[28] The Party also purged many members suspected of corruption. The VCP expelled a total of 86,000 members and simultaneously ushered in a youth movement.[29] Over 90 percent of the 370,000 new Party members selected at the Fifth Congress were under thirty. Seventy percent of these had served in the army during the Second Indochina War.[30] "We were trying to institute a generational change along with an important commitment to the ideals of our revolution," one former Foreign Ministry official recently reported.[31] "We needed to remind our people who had delivered them from the horrors of occupation," stressed another. "We emphasized our Party's revolutionary traditions and accepted new members from the People's Army to illustrate this point."[32]

The promotion of a new generation of Party members from the ranks of the People's Army tells us much about the character of the VCP and the nature of its relationship to the past. Confucianism had always identified itself with the selfless devotion of the masses to the cause of salvation of the fatherland. The VCP capitalized on this patriarchal relationship by replacing the mandarin as the father of the people. Interestingly, the VCP's official name for its conflict with the United States is not "the American War," as is often reported in the West, but rather *Cuoc khang chien chong My, cuu nuoc* (the great anti-U.S. resistance war for national salvation of the fatherland).

In the postwar period, however, the people wondered whether the Party truly had the mandate from heaven, that is, the right to rule by heaven's will.[33] These doubts forced VCP leaders to continually stress past accomplishments instead of current practices to win favor with the peasants. "We began to question the authority of the Party," one farmer said in 1996. "We could not understand their policies."[34] Bui Tin, a former PAVN officer and editor of *Nhan Dan,* explains postwar criticism of the Party this way: "During the tension of the war all decision-making was concentrated in the hands of a few men and they had become over-confident. They simply assumed that since people had always supported them in opposing foreign aggression, they themselves were immune to criticism."[35] The right of a particular group to hold political authority had always been open to question in Vietnam. By the mid-1980s, because of severe economic problems and charges of corruption, the VCP was in a precarious position.

As the Party relied more heavily upon its past revolutionary victories for political legitimacy, great changes threatened the future of the socialist experiment. The forced collectivization of the late 1970s had given way by the mid-1980s to a more pragmatic political and economic course aimed at ending stagnation and introducing rapid economic growth. In 1986, the VCP liberalized the economy, allowing joint ventures and export industries to establish a foothold throughout Vietnam. The Party also allowed small-scale capitalist enterprises to supply the state with needed resources and to compete with state products. Furthermore, the economic reforms diminished the role of state subsidies. These economic changes, while partly a result of the Soviet Union's new policies, were also driven by events within Vietnam itself. *Doi moi* (renovation) was made possible only by the successful transfer of power to a second generation of revolutionary leaders. This change took place in the decade between the Fourth National Congress in 1976 and the Sixth National Congress in 1986, and was precipitated by Le Duan's death.

Le Duan had served the Communist Party as its secretary since 1960, and his death in the summer of 1986 set in motion a series of events that eventually led to a dramatic change in thinking in Hanoi. "Le Duan was a fossil," one Party leader declared confidentially. "He had no vision and knew little of the changing world around him."[36] Bui Tin complained, "Very few of Le Duan's initiatives in rebuilding the country were actually worthwhile."[37] For nearly a decade before his death, Le Duan had been the subject of severe criticism, and his passing marked the beginning of the end for "the old way of thinking."[38] At the Sixth National Congress in December 1986, the VCP replaced most of its first generation of leaders. Truong Chinh, Pham Van Dong, and Le Duc Tho gave up their seats on the Political Bureau. Tho sent a letter to his two comrades urging them to support the change. He wrote, "I consider this to be a reasonable idea. If all three of us continue to occupy our positions, we might be suspected of wishing to hang on to power."[39] In keeping with the revolutionary tradition, however, this group formed a Council of Elders who participated regularly in Political Bureau meetings. One year later, in 1987, Pham Hung replaced Pham Van Dong as prime minister; Dong had served for thirty-two consecutive years. Hung was the last of the first generation of Party leaders to remain in power.

The Party selected Nguyen Van Linh as the new secretary-general, just five years after he had been ousted from the Party for his liberal economic views. Linh was a southerner and the first of what appeared to be a "southern wind" that took over the political reins in Hanoi. He was a strong advocate for political reform, but within the Party's clearly defined leadership role. In an editorial in *Nhan Dan,* the Party's daily newspaper, he suggested that readers respond more vigorously to government shortcomings and make greater demands on the Party. He released all political prisoners in 1988 and encouraged intellectuals and artists to express themselves freely. In a dramatic departure from past practice, Linh announced that the VCP would give district and provincial leaders the opportunity to discuss policy issues with their constituents before they were enacted at a plenum.[40] In addition, at the Sixth National Congress, the number of candidates for the Central Committee was greater than the number of seats for the first time in the Party's history.[41]

In recent years, however, political observers have noticed an increased entrenchment within the VCP. As Hanoi moves slowly toward economic liberalization, especially in the export sector, the Party has simultaneously slowed the pace of political reform. Even Nguyen Van Linh backed away from political change, reasserting the Party's dictatorship over the proletariat in the wake of the Tiananmen Square demonstrations in Beijing. In a speech before the Central Committee in August 1989, he declared that democracy "does not mean that one is free to write or say what one wants to write or say."[42] One year later, the Party dismissed Political Bureau member Tran Xuan Bach for his unyielding support of political reform. In 1991, Senior General Tran Van Tra was removed from his seat in the National Assembly, presumably for his criticism of VCP policies. In 1989, Tra had formed the Club of Former Resistance Fighters, which openly criticized the Party for its conservative and reactionary practices. He called for greater political and economic reform and demanded anti-corruption laws. Even with internal pressures mounting against it, the VCP had no intention of loosening its grip on the political process. As William Duiker has pointed out, democracy Vietnamese-style is still about the form of participation, not choice.[43]

In the face of mounting opposition from domestic rivals, the VCP has again used its role in leading the country to independence to solidify its hold on political power. After a substantial drop in the 1980s, the military's participation in the Central Committee and Political Bureau has increased dramatically. "We need to remind our critics that we would still be in chains if it were not for the correct leadership of the Party," one VCP official said.[44] Another military leader recently commented, "The Party's leading revolutionary heroes have handled every situation they faced. First it was the French, then the Japanese, and then the Americans invaded our shores. After all this, can't we believe that the Party knows what is best?"[45] The VCP has always maintained that the "people lead and the Party follows," but the continued use of revolutionary slogans and official Communist organs to promote political fidelity suggests otherwise.

The VCP's two most recent selections for secretary-general also represent the Party's increasing reliance on its ties to a glorious past. Do Muoi took over the post in 1991, promising to keep Vietnam on the road to reform. "Do Muoi wanted the Party to continue along its socialist trajectory while he preached reform," one Central Committee member recently reported in confidence. "He used his role in the revolution to advance outdated and outmoded revolutionary ideals."[46] Do Muoi did cast himself as a reformer, but also proclaimed that he wanted the vast economic changes taking place to "build up socialism more effectively, not to renounce socialism."[47] Most critics saw his selection for the Party's highest office as a direct message to Prime Minister Vo Van Kiet and his group of reform-minded supporters. Some Party officials had long feared that Kiet wanted to go too far along the path of political reform.

"He threatened the Party's primary role in the lives of the people," one critic noted, "and this made him a dangerous man."[48]

These first stirrings of ideological pluralism persist within the Party, even as it continues to select "true believers" for important positions. In 1996, at its Eighth National Congress, the VCP chose Le Kha Phieu to replace the aging Do Muoi as secretary-general. Phieu came to the Party's top spot through the military, having served as a general in the People's Army for more than three decades. General Phieu was also the director of the Military-Political Department within the army's own organizational apparatus. One former Party official, a leading reformer, said in 1996, "General Phieu's selection as secretary-general is a conservative reaction against the progressive forces who are pushing for change in Hanoi."[49] Another critic warns, however, "Don't let the debate within the Party fool you . . . the VCP is not about to allow opposition groups to form."[50] This may be sage advice, as the Party has no plans to relinquish control.

Continuity has marked the Party's leadership philosophy for the past seventy years. However, growing voices of protest are emerging outside the corridors of power in Hanoi. Recent demonstrations in rural provinces over rice allocation and subsidies have included political critiques of the government. "We don't understand these ancient Party leaders," commented one student leader in Hue. "They speak of a revolution that means nothing to the young people of Vietnam."[51] Indeed, half of Vietnam's population of 74 million has been born since the fall of Saigon in 1975. "The political leadership is out of touch with the young people," one student from Hanoi recently complained. "They do not represent our goals, dreams, or aspirations."[52]

Several of Vietnam's most respected scholars have also joined the attack against the government. Nguyen Khac Vien, Vietnam's most important contemporary historian, spent the last years of his life condemning the government he had helped establish. In a report to the Western press, Professor Vien declared the Party leadership "totally impotent" and "incapable of following the changing times." He urged the VCP to establish "broad-based rules for democracy" or face an uncertain future in which Vietnam "stands alone . . . unable to compete with its neighbors."[53] Bui Tin, former PAVN officer and editor of the Party's official daily newspaper, has recently defected so that he can "make public a growing list of personal misgivings about Vietnam and its political system."[54] In his 1995 memoir, Tin criticized the Party's political leadership and called for a participatory democracy.[55]

Another significant challenge to the VCP's revolutionary authority has come from writers living inside Vietnam. Vietnam's tradition of literature as a form of political protest has deep historic roots, and scholars should not ignore its impact on contemporary society. According to one expert, "literature is the most potent form for the public exchange of ideas in Vietnam today."[56] Several important writers have emerged in the last decade who have criticized the Party's authority and even the wisdom of the war itself.

Of all the fiction writers in Vietnam today, Duong Thu Huong and Bao Ninh are perhaps the best known. They are concerned with real-life circumstances in a Vietnam where many of the protagonists are without power to alter the events that influence their lives. They tend to write about topics that generally fall within the realm of the VCP and its "court historians": heroism and Vietnam's glorious past. The Party, of course, has maintained careful control over history and the national narrative, dragging up heroes from yesteryear to illustrate continuity with the past and to confer legitimacy on its own heroes. The VCP has responded harshly to criticism by literary figures, placing several authors under house arrest and confiscating books shortly after publication. What seems to upset Party officials most is the ability of the fiction writer to discredit the pantheon of heroes put forth by the VCP by blurring the line between fiction and history.

Ironically, what makes Ninh and Huong so important to a contemporary Vietnamese audience is their own wartime experience. Ninh served with the Glorious 27th Youth Brigade during the Second Indochina War. Of the 500 who went to fight with the brigade in 1969, he is one of ten survivors. Huong spent seven years at the front in a Communist youth brigade; she was one of only three survivors of a unit of forty men and women.[57] During the 1979 war with China, she was the first woman combatant present at the front lines. The VCP expelled her in 1989, and in 1991 placed her under house arrest. She remains a controversial figure in Hanoi today and continues to challenge the VCP's rigid political system.

In their writings, Huong and Ninh have assigned all-too-human characteristics to Vietnam's national heroes. These characters all have feet of clay and are subject to the same vagaries of everyday life as other citizens. Huong and Ninh have also asked whether the huge sacrifice of the war was worth it to achieve unification. In Ninh's 1991 novel *The Sorrow of War,* his protagonist, Kien, questions the meaning of the long and costly war as he struggles to write about all that he has witnessed. Kien writes of individuals powerless and alone, not cadre-heroes out to save the fatherland.[58] In her most powerful novel, *Paradise of the Blind,* Huong tells the story of a corrupt Party official who is quick to criticize Vietnam's youth. She writes, "Where does it all come from, your need to humiliate us. In the name of what? You say our dances are decadent, but haven't you done some dancing yourself?"[59] And in her pathbreaking *Novel without a Name,* Huong's central character has doubts about his patriotism and the Party's long war. Quan, a platoon leader with the People's Army, is on leave when the disillusionment begins. "We were drunk on our youth," he remembers, "marching toward a glorious future because history was on our side."[60]

Perhaps the most important challenge to the Party's legitimacy, however, has come from various Buddhist groups. During the war, Buddhist religious leaders were central figures in the protest against the Saigon regime, and many Vietnamese looked to them as a possible "third force" with legitimate social and political power.[61]

Although the National Liberation Front had infiltrated many Buddhist groups, individual temples and monks remained out of reach for Hanoi and Saigon. The self-immolation of Thich Quang Duc in 1963 remains a powerful image in Vietnam today and offers a direct challenge to the Party's monopoly on revolutionary heroism. "When I think of great sacrifice for the country's good," a young Saigon student recently explained, "I think of the Buddhist protest against corruption and injustice . . . not the Communists."[62] Another believes that "the Buddhists, not the Party, represent the best of Vietnam yesterday and today."[63]

Young people in Hanoi and the northern provinces share this view. An office worker in Haiphong observed, "The Party claims it is the leader, the vanguard, and that only its wise leaders could lead the country in war and in peace. This is not true. Our Buddhist monks predate the Party, and they will be here long after the Communists are nothing but footnotes in history books."[64] A young student from one of Hanoi's technical colleges stressed that Vietnam "has a long history, and the Party will quickly fade into the background. Buddhism, on the other hand, is a way of life for many Vietnamese. We appreciate the sacrifices Buddhists have made throughout our history and look to them as our real heroes."[65]

In the postwar period, the Buddhists have resurfaced as a viable political force. Cultivating their own image of past sacrifice for the good of the nation, Buddhist leaders have once again led the protest against the central government. At first, the Party did not know how to respond to this new crisis, so it struck out with brute force. In April 1977, internal security police carried out raids on the An Quang pagoda, capturing several of its leaders, including Thich Quang Do and Thich Huyen Quang. The government tried the two for "working against the revolution, sabotaging the people's solidarity bloc, counterrevolutionary propaganda, and exploiting religion to undermine security and order."[66] They were eventually acquitted, but were recaptured in February 1982 and placed under house arrest in their native villages in central Vietnam.

To stem the tide of Buddhist protests, the Party created its own officially sanctioned religion, "Vietnam's Buddhist Church." Few in Vietnam recognized the new church, however, and the protests continued. In 1982 and again in 1983, the Party arrested several leaders of the Unified Buddhist Church. In April 1984, security police raided two temples in Ho Chi Minh City and arrested nearly twenty monks and nuns. Among those held were Thich Tue Sy and Thich Tri Sieu, two of the most important antigovernment activists in the south. Both were kept in solitary confinement during their trial, and eventually the state condemned them to death. When the streets filled with protesters, the Party commuted their sentence to twenty years' imprisonment. According to one published survey, Hanoi continues to hold several Buddhist leaders in reeducation camps, their "home" since the war's end.[67]

Hanoi's crackdown has done little to slow Buddhist attacks, however, and the Party faces a difficult road ahead if it plans to battle the monks and nuns for the mandate of heaven. "Millions of Vietnamese see Buddhism as the one constant in our struggle against foreigners," a leading intellectual recently reported, "and no amount of political posturing is going to change this pervasive attitude."[68] The Buddhists do share the mantle of revolutionary heroism with the Party, and many think their hands are less bloody than those of the leaders in Hanoi. According to one young university student, "The Buddhists fought for peace while the Communists marched blindly forward following a path of destruction."[69] This is a popular view in present-day Vietnam, especially among young people in the countryside. Whatever the future holds for the Party, it will surely have to reconcile with the Buddhists.

The struggle to own the past will no doubt play a large role in Vietnam's political future. The Party's monopoly on political power has, in many ways, depended upon its ability to promote itself as the vanguard of a social movement that brought Vietnam freedom and independence. Vietnam's Confucian and Buddhist traditions paved the way for the VCP's brand of paternal socialism, and Party leaders have been quick to point to social continuity for support of their revolution. In the postwar period, the VCP's bureaucratic structure ensured that no single individual would gain a preponderance of power, but it also limited political participation to the Party's revolutionary elite.[70] In recent years, the first signs of ideological conflict within the VCP caused a dramatic return to emphasis on revolutionary heroism, and, as a result, the military has gained increased political power.

For Vietnam to move forward, it will have to break the cult of solidarity that has gripped the Party since the Third National Congress in 1960. Because the VCP has condemned "peaceful evolution" as a worn-out trick of Western capitalist nations, the future seems unclear. What is clear, however, is that the Party will have to allow people greater participation in the political process if it hopes to build popular support. Having led the country in a century-long resistance struggle is, evidently, not enough.

Reflections on War in the Twenty-first Century

■

ROBERT S. MCNAMARA

Robert S. McNamara served as Secretary of Defense from January 1961 to February 1968. Initially he was an advocate of American escalation in Vietnam, but as the war lengthened and became stalemated, McNamara sought to limit the American military commitment there and to pursue a negotiated end to the struggle. For many years he declined to discuss his role in the war, but in 1995 he published *In Retrospect: The Tragedy and Lessons of Vietnam,* a thorough analysis of high-level decision making and the lessons of the war. McNamara's catalogue of errors that he and other American leaders made in dealing with the Vietnam War is large, ranging from erroneous geopolitical assumptions, to an ignorance of Vietnamese history, culture, and politics, to a failure to inform properly the American people and Congress, to a misunderstanding of the limits of a modern, high-technology army, to an arrogance and can-do spirit that ignored the frailties of political leaders and the intractability of many foreign policy problems.

Convinced that the Vietnam War might have been prevented or ended before it ran its course, McNamara was instrumental in the formation of the Vietnam War Project at Brown University. As part of this effort to bring together scholars and participants from both sides, McNamara traveled to Hanoi in November 1995 (the highest-ranking former American official to do so) and in June 1997 attended a large conference there. In 1999 he and four collaborators published *Argument Without End: In Search of Answers to the Vietnam Tragedy,* an ambitious effort to identify "missed opportunities" of the Vietnam War and to use the lessons of the past to instruct contemporary policymakers. "Now is the time," McNamara writes in the book, "to face our past together so that those who follow us can learn from our experiences" (p. 391). In the essay that follows, he moves beyond the Vietnam War to a broader consideration of issues of war and peace in the next century.

C. E. N.

■

I want to begin my remarks by telling you of my earliest memory as a child. It is of a city exploding with joy. The city was San Francisco. The date was November 11, 1918—Armistice Day. I was two years old. The city was celebrating not only the end of World War I, but the belief, held so strongly by President Woodrow Wilson and by many other Americans, that the United States and its allies had won a war to end all wars.

They were wrong, of course. The twentieth century was on its way to becoming the bloodiest, by far, in all of human history: during its span, 160 million people will have been killed in conflicts—within nations and between nations—across the globe. Were similar conflicts to take place in the twenty-first century, when population will have risen threefold and when wars are likely to be fought with weapons of mass destruction, fatalities would be substantially higher—at least 300 million.

Is that what we want in the first century of the new millennium?

I hope not.

If not, the time to initiate action to prevent that tragedy is now.

We should begin by establishing a realistic appraisal of the problem. It is readily apparent, very complex, and very dangerous.

The Carnegie Commission stated it clearly when it said:

> Peace—will require greater understanding and respect for differences within and across national boundaries. We humans do not have the luxury any longer of indulging our prejudices and ethnocentrism. They are anachronisms of our ancient past. The worldwide historical record is full of hateful and destructive behavior based on religious, racial, political, ideological, and other distinctions—holy wars of one sort or another. Will such behavior in the next century be expressed with weapons of mass destruction? If we cannot learn to accommodate each other respectfully in the twenty-first century, we could destroy each other at such a rate that humanity will have little to cherish.[1]

The Commission is saying, in effect, that the end of the Cold War in 1989 did not and will not, in and of itself, result in an end to conflict. We see evidence of the truth of that statement on all sides: the Iraqi invasion of Kuwait, the civil war in the former Yugoslavia, the turmoil in northern Iraq, the tension between India and Pakistan, the unstable relations between North and South Korea, and the conflicts across the face of sub-Saharan Africa, in Somalia, Sudan, Rwanda, Burundi, Zaire, Sierra Leone, and Liberia. These all make clear that the world of the future will not be without conflict, conflict between disparate groups within nations and conflict extending across national borders. Racial, religious, and ethnic tensions will remain. Nationalism will be a powerful force across the globe. Political revolutions will erupt as societies advance. Historic disputes over political boundaries will endure. And economic disparities among and within nations will increase as technology and education spread unevenly around the world. The underlying causes of Third World conflict that existed long before the Cold War began remain now that it has ended. They will be compounded by potential strife among states of the former Soviet Union and by continuing tensions in the Middle East. It is just such tensions that in the past fifty years have contributed to 125 wars causing 40 million deaths.

So, in these respects, the world of the future will not be different from the world of the past—conflicts within nations and conflicts among nations will not disappear. But relations between nations will change dramatically. In the post–World War II years, the United States had the power—and to a considerable degree we exercised that power—to shape the world as we chose. In the next century, that will not be possible.

Japan is destined to play a larger role on the world scene, exercising greater economic and political power and, one hopes, assuming greater economic and political responsibility. The same can be said of Western Europe, following its major step toward economic integration.

And by the middle of the next century, several of the countries of what in the past we have termed the Third World will have grown so dramatically in population and economic power as to become major forces in international relations. India is likely to have a population of 1.6 billion; Nigeria, 400 million; Brazil, 300 million. And if China achieves its ambitious economic goals for the year 2000 (they are likely to be exceeded) and then maintains satisfactory but not spectacular growth rates for the next fifty years, its 1.6 billion people will have the income of Western Europeans in the 1960s. It will indeed be a power to be reckoned with—economically, politically, and militarily.

These figures are, of course, highly speculative. I point to them simply to emphasize the magnitude and pace of the changes that lie ahead and the need now to adjust our goals, our policies, and our institutions to take account of them. In particular, they should make clear that neither the United States nor Japan has even begun to adjust its foreign policy to relate properly to the China it will face in our children's lifetime.

While remaining the world's strongest nation, in the next century the United States will live in a multipolar world, and its foreign policy and defense programs must be adjusted to this emerging reality. In such a world, a need clearly exists for developing new relationships both among the great powers and between the great powers and other nations.

Many political theorists, in particular those classified as "realists," predict a return to traditional power politics. They argue that the disappearance of the ideological competition between East and West will trigger a reversion to traditional relationships based on territorial and economic imperatives. They say that the United States, Russia, Western Europe, China, Japan, and perhaps India will seek to assert themselves in their own regions while still competing for dominance in other areas of the world where conditions are fluid. This view has been expressed by, for example, Harvard professor Michael Sandel:

> The end of the Cold War does not mean an end of global competition between the Superpowers. Once the ideological dimension fades, what you are left with is not peace and harmony, but old-fashioned global politics based on dominate powers competing for influence and pursuing their internal interests.[2]

Henry Kissinger, also a member of the realist school, has expressed a similar conclusion:

> Victory in the Cold War has propelled America into a world which bears many similarities to the European state system of the eighteenth and nineteenth centuries. . . . The absence of both an overriding ideological or strategic threat frees nations to pursue foreign policies based increasingly on their immediate national interest. In an international system characterized by perhaps five or six major powers and a multiplicity of smaller states, order will have to emerge much as it did in past centuries from a reconciliation and balancing of competing national interests.[3]

In contrast to Sandel and Kissinger, Carl Kaysen, former director of the Institute of Advanced Studies at Princeton, has written:

> The International system that relies on the national use of military force as the ultimate guarantor of security, and the threat of its use as the basis of order, is not the only possible one. To seek a different

system . . . is no longer the pursuit of an illusion, but a necessary effort toward a necessary goal.[4]

Kissinger's and Sandel's conceptions of relations among nations in the post–Cold War world are, of course, historically well founded, but I would argue that they are inconsistent with our increasingly interdependent world. No nation, not even the United States, can stand alone in a world in which nations are inextricably entwined with one another economically, environmentally, and with regard to security. I believe, therefore, that for the future, the United Nations charter offers a far more appropriate framework for international relations than does the doctrine of power politics.

I would argue also that Kissinger's and Sandel's emphasis on balance-of-power politics in the twenty-first century assumes we will be willing to continue to accept a foreign policy that lacks a strong moral foundation. I am aware that the majority of political scientists, particularly those who are members of the political realist school, believe that morality—as contrasted to a careful calculation of national interests based on balance-of-power considerations—is a dangerous guide for the establishment of foreign policy. They would say that a foreign policy driven by moral considerations promotes zealousness and a crusading spirit, with potentially dangerous results.

But surely, in the most basic sense, one can apply a moral judgment to the level of killing that occurred in the twentieth century. There can be no justification for it. Nor can there be any justification for its continuation into the twenty-first century. On moral grounds alone, we should act today to prevent such an outcome. A first step would be to establish such an objective as the primary foreign policy goal both for our own nation and for the entire human race.

The United States has defined itself in highly idealistic and moral terms throughout its history. We have seen ourselves as defenders of human freedoms across the globe. That feeling was the foundation of Woodrow Wilson's support for normative rules of international behavior to be administered by a League of Nations. Our moral vision has had an impact on the world. It has led to the formation of a score of international institutions in the economic, social, and political fields. But it remains under attack—both within and outside the United States—by those who put greater weight on considerations of narrow national interest.

And many of the most controversial foreign policy debates have found both sides basing their arguments on moral considerations. American policy toward Cuba today is justified on moral grounds by its supporters, who say it is immoral to support dictators who abuse human rights. And it is attacked, on moral grounds, by its critics, who say it leads to suffering by the mass of the Cuban people. Similarly, a U.S. policy toward China that placed primary emphasis on support of individual civil rights might well weaken the Chinese government's ability to increase the access of the mass of its population to advances in nutrition, education, and health.

Nor do moral considerations offer a clear guide to action in many other foreign policy disputes—for example, the conflicts today in the Middle East or in Serbia. And even where the moral objective may be clear, we may lack the capability to achieve it. We are learning that external military force has limited power to restore a failed state.

Moreover, peoples of different religions and different cultures, confronting common problems, often arrive at different moral judgments relating to conflicts between individual and group rights, between group rights and national rights, and between the rights of individual nations.

So, while most Americans accept the proposition that our foreign policy should advance the welfare of peoples across the globe in terms of political freedom, freedom from want, and preservation of the environment, those objectives are so general that they provide little guidance to addressing the problems that a government confronts each day.

But can we not agree that there is one area of foreign policy in which moral principles should prevail and in which they have not? And that is in relation to the settlement of disputes within nations and among nations without resort to violence.

If so, three specific steps are required:

1. We should reduce the risk of conflict within and among nations by establishing a system of collective security[5] that would have two objectives: the prevention of war and the termination of conflict in the event deterrence fails.

2. The system of collective security should place particular emphasis on limiting the risk of war between or among great powers.

3. To avoid the risk of the destruction of nations in the event collective security breaks down, we should redouble our efforts to eliminate weapons of mass destruction, particularly nuclear weapons.

The collective security regime should:

1. Provide all states collective guarantees against external aggression—frontiers would not be changed by force.

2. Codify the rights of minorities and ethnic groups within states—the rights of Muslims in Bosnia, for example—and provide a process by which such groups who believe their rights have been violated may seek redress without resort to violence.

3. Establish a mechanism for resolution of both regional conflicts and conflicts within nations, without unilateral action by the great powers. Military force, other than in defense of national territory, would be used only multilaterally, in accordance with agreed-upon norms.

In sum, I believe we should strive to move toward a world in which relations among nations would be based on the rule of law, a world in which the conflict-resolution and peacekeeping functions necessary to accomplish these objectives would be performed by multilateral organizations—a reorganized and strengthened United Nations and new and expanded regional organizations.

That is my vision of a system of collective security for the twenty-first century.

Such a vision is easier to articulate than to achieve. The goal is clear; but how to get there is not. And I have no magic formula, no simple road map to success. I do know that such a vision will not be achieved in a month, a year, or even a decade. It will be achieved, if at all, slowly and through small steps, by leaders of dedication and persistence. So I urge that we begin that process now.

Such a world will need leaders. The leadership role may shift among nations depending on the issue at hand. But more often than not, no other nation than the United States will be capable of filling that role. However, we cannot succeed in such an endeavor without the cooperation of other nations. And we will not receive that cooperation if we continue to act as though we were omniscient. We are not.

And yet over and over again—as with respect to Vietnam, Cuba, Iran, and Iraq—we act as though we think we are. Failing to obtain the endorsement of other nations, we have applied our power unilaterally. My belief is that the United States should never apply its economic, political, or military power other than in a multilateral context. The single exception would be in the highly unlikely case of a direct threat to the security of the continental United States, Alaska, or Hawaii.

Whenever the United States accepts leadership in such a multilateral context, it must accept collective decision-making—a concept our people are neither accustomed to nor comfortable with. And other nations—certainly including Japan—must accept a sharing of the risks and costs: the political risks, the financial costs, and the risks of casualties. If the casualties in the Persian Gulf War had been as great as the Joint Chiefs of Staff had originally forecast, 90 percent of the "blood cost" would have been borne by us, while by far the greater part of the benefits—in the form of assured petroleum supply—would have accrued to other nations.

Had the United States and other major powers made clear their commitment to such a system of collective security, and had they stated they would protect nations against attack, the 1990 Iraqi invasion of Kuwait might well have been deterred. Similarly, had the United Nations or NATO taken action when conflict in the former Yugoslavia erupted in the early 1990s, the ensuing slaughter of tens of thousands of innocent victims might have been prevented.

In the post–Cold War world, operating under a system of collective security, nations—and in particular the great powers—should be clear about where, and how, they would apply military force. They clearly cannot and should not intervene in every conflict leading to the slaughter of innocent civilians. More than a dozen wars currently rage throughout the world. And other serious conflicts may soon break out elsewhere. Where, if at all, should the great powers and/or the United Nations be involved? Neither the United States nor any other great power has a clear answer to this question. The answers can be developed only through intense debate, over a period of years, within our own nation, among the other great powers, and in the councils of international organizations.

The rules governing response to aggression across national borders can be relatively simple and clear. But those relating to attempts to maintain or restore political order and to prevent wholesale slaughter within nations are far less so.

Criteria determining the use of American military forces should be derived from a precise statement of our foreign policy objectives. For forty years, our objective remained clear: to contain an expansionist Soviet Union. But that can no longer be the focus of our efforts. We have lost our enemy. What will we put in its place? President Clinton told the UN General Assembly on September 27, 1993: "Our overriding purpose must be to expand and strengthen the world's community of market-based democracies."[6] Anthony

Lake, his National Security Adviser, echoed this a short time later when he stated that "the successor to a doctrine of containment must be a strategy of enlargement—enlargement of the world's free community of market democracies." Such a general formulation of our objectives is not sufficient.

The United States cannot and should not intervene in every conflict arising from a nation's attempt to move toward capitalist democracy. For example, we were surely correct not to support with military force Eduard Shevardnadze's attempt to install democracy in Georgia. Nor can we be expected to try to stop by military force every instance of the slaughter of innocent civilians.

Several crucial questions must be faced. To what degree of human suffering should we respond? Under a UN convention formalized in a global treaty in 1989, the United States agreed to join in stopping genocide. But what constitutes genocide? In June 1994, the American government, while recognizing the killing of over 200,000 Rwandans as "acts of genocide," refused to state that the killing fell under the treaty's provisions.[7] And would not other cases, short of genocide, also justify intervention? At what point should we intervene—as preventive diplomacy fails and killing appears likely, or only when the slaughter is increasing? How should we respond when nations involved in such conflicts claim that outside intervention clearly infringes on their sovereignty, as was the case in the former Yugoslavia? We have seen regional organizations—in particular, the Organization of African Unity and the Organization of American States—time and time again fail to support such intervention.

Above all else, the criteria governing intervention should recognize a lesson we should have learned in Vietnam: external military force has only a limited capacity to facilitate the process of nation building.

It should be made clear to our people that such questions will, at best, require years to answer. But we should force the debate within our own nation and within international forums. Some of the issues may never be resolved. There may be times when we must recognize that we cannot right all wrongs.

If we are to achieve the objective of avoiding in the twenty-first century the tragic loss of life we have just witnessed, then above all else, special emphasis must be placed on avoiding conflict among the great powers.

Excluding the end of the Cold War, I believe the two most important geopolitical events of the past fifty years have been the reconciliation between France and Germany, after centuries of enmity, and the establishment of peaceful relations between Japan and the United States, after one of the bloodiest conflicts in the modern era. It is inconceivable today that either Germany or Japan would engage in war with any of the great powers of the Western world. Can we not move to integrate both Russia and China into the family of nations in ways that make war between them and the other great powers equally unlikely?

We have not done so.

The expansion of NATO is viewed by many Russian leaders as a threat to their nation's security. At a time when their nation's military forces—both conventional and nuclear—have been severely weakened, they see NATO planning to move its forces to their western borders. This has strengthened the position of their hard-line nationalists, increased their feelings of xenophobia, and, through the scrapping of their doctrine of "no first use," led to a more aggressive nuclear policy. George F. Kennan has stated that NATO expansion will prove to be one of the greatest foreign policy mistakes made by the West since the end of World War II.[8] I agree with him.

Similarly, China has viewed the action taken in 1997 by America and Japan to extend—and, in the words of the Chinese, "to expand"—the United States–Japan Security Treaty as a hostile act. In 1997, Prime Minister Li Peng stated very emphatically to me and my associates during a visit to his country that whereas initially the treaty might have been directed against the Soviet Union, with the end of the Cold War it could have no purpose other than to contain and, ultimately, threaten China. He argued that, contrary to the action of Germany, Japan had never admitted or accepted responsibility for its role in World War II. He claimed—perhaps with exaggeration—that Japan was responsible for 20 million Chinese dead. And he said he observed continuing signs of militarism in Japanese society.

Dangerous frustrations also exist between China and the United States arising from divergent policies toward Taiwan, North Korea, and the East Asia region.

My associates and I were shocked by the vehemence with which the Chinese stated their views. I mention them here to illustrate how far both we and the Japanese have to go before we can establish a pattern of relations with China comparable to those that exist between France and Germany and between the United States and Japan.

I turn now to the third of the three actions to which I urge immediate attention be directed: action to avoid the risk of destruction of nations, through the use of weapons of mass destruction—in particular, nuclear weapons—in the event that collective security breaks down.

Today, nine years after the end of the Cold War, approximately 40,000 nuclear warheads are in the world, with a destructive power more than 1 million times greater than the bomb that flattened Hiroshima. Americans—and all other inhabitants of our globe—continue to live with the risk of nuclear destruction. The United States' war plans provide for contingent use of nuclear weapons, just as they did when I was Secretary of Defense in the 1960s. But I do not believe that the average American recognizes this fact. No doubt, he or she was surprised and pleased by the announcement of the Start I nuclear arms control treaty, which was signed by the United States and Russia in 1991. When finally implemented, it will reduce the arsenal to approximately 20,000 weapons. In June

1992, Presidents George Bush and Boris Yeltsin agreed to Start II, which would further reduce the total, to 10,000. In March 1997, Presidents Clinton and Yeltsin spoke of going still lower, to a level of 6,000. But Start II has not been and may never be ratified.

Moreover, even if that agreement, and the further reductions discussed in 1997, were to be approved by Congress and the Duma, the risk of destruction of societies across the globe, while somewhat reduced, would be far from eliminated. I doubt that a survivor—if there were one—could perceive much difference between a world in which 6,000 nuclear warheads had been exploded and one subject to attack by 40,000. So the question is, can we not go further? Surely the answer must be yes.

The end of the Cold War, along with the growing understanding of the lack of utility of nuclear weapons and of the high risk associated with their continued existence, points to both the opportunity and the urgency with which the nuclear powers should reexamine their long-term nuclear force objectives. We should begin with a broad public debate over alternative nuclear strategies. I believe such a debate should open with a discussion of the moral issues relating to the use of nuclear weapons by the five declared nuclear powers.

As I stated earlier, most political scientists and most security experts oppose introducing moral considerations into discussions of international relations and defense policy. And I will admit that in many situations such considerations provide ambiguous guidance at best. But surely the human race should be prepared to accept the fact that it is totally immoral for one nation, no matter what the provocation, to believe that it—through its leader, acting alone—has the right to initiate action that will destroy another nation. And would it not be even more morally unacceptable if such action by one belligerent would destroy not only the other belligerent, but—through the spread of radioactive fallout—nonbelligerent nations across the globe as well? Yet that would have been the result if either

Russia or the United States had implemented the nuclear strategy that each nation followed for forty years and continues to follow today.

The debate should then move beyond moral considerations to a detailed examination of the military utility of nuclear weapons and the offsetting military risks of their use. I believe it would support the conclusion that we should move back to a nonnuclear world.

In support of my position, I will make three points:

1. The experience of the Cuban missile crisis in 1962—and, in particular, what has been learned about it recently—makes clear that so long as we and other great powers possess large inventories of nuclear weapons, we will face the risk of their use and the destruction of our nation.

2. That risk is no longer justifiable on military grounds—if it ever was.

3. In recent years, the thinking of leading Western security experts, both military and civilian, regarding the military utility of nuclear weapons has changed dramatically. More and more of them—although certainly not yet a majority—are expressing views similar to those I have stated.

First, the Cuban missile crisis.

It is now widely recognized that the actions of the Soviet Union, Cuba, and the United States in October 1962 brought the three nations to the verge of war. But what was not known then, and is not widely understood today, was how close the world came to the brink of nuclear disaster. In 1997 the release of highly classified tapes by the Kennedy Library provided new insights into the near catastrophe from an American point of view.[9] The same year, a similar account of Nikita Khrushchev's state of mind was published.[10] Both accounts are frightening. Neither the Soviet Union nor the United States intended, by its actions, to create the risks they both incurred.

The crisis began when the Soviets moved nuclear missiles and bombers to Cuba—secretly and with the clear intent to deceive—in the summer and early fall of 1962. The missiles were to be targeted against cities along America's East Coast, putting 90 million Americans at risk. Photographs taken by a U-2 reconnaissance aircraft on Sunday, October 14, 1962, brought the deployments to President Kennedy's attention. He and his military and civilian security advisers believed that the Soviets' action posed a threat to the West. Kennedy therefore authorized a naval quarantine of Cuba, to be effective Wednesday, October 24. Preparations also began for air strikes and an amphibious invasion. The contingency plans called for a huge "first-day" air attack of 1,080 sorties. An invasion force totaling 180,000 troops was assembled in Southeastern ports. The crisis came to a head on Saturday, October 27, and Sunday, October 28. Had Khrushchev not publicly announced on that Sunday that he was removing the missiles, I believe that on Monday, a majority of Kennedy's military and civilian advisers would have recommended launching the attacks.

To understand what caused the crisis—and how to avoid similar ones in the future—high-ranking Soviet, Cuban, and American participants met in a series of conferences beginning in 1987. The meetings extended over a period of five years. The one chaired by Fidel Castro in Havana in January 1992 was the fifth and last.

By the conclusion of the third meeting, in Moscow, it had become clear that the decisions of each of the three nations, before and during the crisis, had been distorted by misinformation, miscalculation, and misjudgment. I shall cite only four of many examples:

1. Before Soviet missiles were introduced into Cuba in the summer of 1962, the Soviet Union and Cuba believed that the United States intended to invade the island in order to overthrow Castro and remove his government. But we had no such intention.

2. The United States believed that the Soviets would never move

nuclear warheads outside the Soviet Union—they never had before—but in fact, they did. In Moscow, in 1989, we learned that by October 1962, although the CIA at the time was reporting no nuclear weapons on the island, Soviet nuclear warheads had indeed been delivered to Cuba. As I have said, they were to be targeted on American cities.

3. The Soviets believed that nuclear weapons could be introduced into Cuba secretly, without detection, and that the United States would not respond when their presence was disclosed. There, too, they were in error.

4. Finally, those who were prepared to urge President Kennedy to destroy the missiles by an air attack that, in all likelihood, would have been followed by an amphibious invasion were almost certainly mistaken in their belief that the Soviets would not respond militarily. At the time, the CIA reported 10,000 Soviet troops in Cuba. At the Moscow conference, we learned that 43,000 Soviet troops were in fact on the island, along with 270,000 well-armed Cuban troops. Both forces, in the words of their commanders, were determined to "fight to the death." The Cuban officials estimated they would have suffered 100,000 casualties. The Soviets—including longtime foreign minister Andrei A. Gromyko and former ambassador to the United States Anatoly Dobrynin—expressed utter disbelief that we could have thought that, in the face of such a catastrophic defeat, they would not have responded militarily somewhere in the world. Very probably, the result would have been uncontrollable escalation.

By the end of that meeting in Moscow, we had agreed we could draw two lessons from our discussions:

1. In the face of nuclear weapons, crisis management is inherently dangerous, difficult, and uncertain.

2. Due to misjudgment, misinformation, and miscalculation of the kind I have referred to, it is not possible to predict with confidence the consequences of military action between great powers

armed with such weapons. Therefore, we must direct our attention and energies to crisis avoidance.

In 1962, during the crisis, some of us—particularly President Kennedy and I—believed the United States faced great danger. The Moscow meeting confirmed that judgment. But during the Havana conference, we learned that the president and I—and certainly others—had seriously underestimated those dangers. While in Havana, we were told by the former Warsaw Pact Chief of Staff, General Anatoly Gribkov, that in 1962, Soviet forces in Cuba possessed not only nuclear warheads for the intermediate-range missiles targeted on American cities, but nuclear bombs and tactical nuclear warheads as well. The tactical warheads were to be used against our invasion forces. At the time, as I mentioned, the CIA was reporting no warheads on the island.

In November 1992—thirty years after the event—we learned more. An article appeared in the Russian press that stated that at the height of the missile crisis, Soviet forces on Cuba possessed a total of 162 nuclear warheads, including at least ninety tactical warheads. Moreover, it was reported that on October 26, 1962—a moment of great tension—warheads were moved from their storage sites to positions closer to their delivery vehicles in anticipation of an American invasion.[11] The next day Soviet Defense Minister Rodion Malinovsky received a cable from General Issa Pliyev, the Soviet commander in Cuba, informing him of this action. Malinovsky sent it to Khrushchev. Khrushchev returned it to Malinovsky with "Approved" scrawled across the document. Clearly, a high risk existed that, in the face of an American attack—which, as I have said, many in the American government, military and civilian alike, were prepared to recommend to President Kennedy—the Soviet forces in Cuba would have decided to use their nuclear weapons rather than lose them.[12]

We need not speculate what would have happened in that event. We can predict the results with certainty.

Although a U.S. invasion force would not have been equipped with tactical nuclear warheads—the president and I had specifically prohibited that—no one should believe that had American troops been attacked with nuclear weapons, the United States would have refrained from a nuclear response. And where would it have ended? In utter disaster.

The point I wish to emphasize is this: human beings are fallible. We know we all make mistakes. In our daily lives, mistakes are costly, but we try to learn from them. In conventional war, they cost lives, sometimes thousands of lives. But if mistakes were to affect decisions relating to the use of nuclear forces, there would be no learning period. They would result in the destruction of nations. I believe, therefore, it can be predicted with confidence that the indefinite combination of human fallibility and nuclear weapons carries a very high risk of potential nuclear catastrophe.[13]

Is there a military justification for continuing to accept that risk? The answer is *no.*

Proponents of nuclear weapons have produced only one plausible scenario for initiating their use: a situation where there is no prospect of retaliation. That means using them either against a nonnuclear state or against one so weakly armed that the user can have full confidence in the capability of its own nuclear forces to achieve a totally disarming first strike. But even such circumstances have not, in fact, provided a sufficient basis for the use of nuclear weapons in war. For example, although American forces were in desperate straits twice during the Korean War—first immediately following the North Korean attack in 1950 and then when the Chinese crossed the Yalu River—the United States did not use nuclear weapons. At that time, North Korea and China had no nuclear capability and the Soviet Union only a negligible one.

The conclusion is clear: the military utility of nuclear weapons is limited to deterring one's opponent from their use.[14] Therefore, if our opponent has no nuclear weapons, we have no need to possess them.

Partly because of the increased understanding of how close we came to disaster during the missile crisis, but also because of a growing recognition of the lack of military utility of the weapons, thinking about the role of nuclear forces has undergone a revolutionary change. Much of this change has occurred in the past five years. Many military leaders are now prepared to go far beyond the Bush-Yeltsin agreement. Some go so far as to state, as I have, that the long-term objective should be a return to a nonnuclear world.[15]

That is, however, a very controversial proposition. A majority of Western security experts—both military and civilian—continue to believe that the threat of the use of nuclear weapons prevents war. Zbigniew Brzezinski, President Carter's National Security Adviser, has argued that a plan for eliminating nuclear weapons "is a plan for making the world safe for conventional warfare. I am therefore not enthusiastic about it."[16] A report of an advisory committee appointed by former Defense Secretary Richard Cheney and chaired by former Air Force Secretary Thomas Reed made essentially the same point. Clearly, the current administration supports that position.[17] Even if one accepts that argument, however, it must be recognized that the deterrent to conventional force aggression carries a very high long-term cost: the risk of a nuclear exchange.

It is that risk—which to me is unacceptable—that is leading prominent security experts to change their views. I doubt that the public is aware of these changes. They have been reflected in numerous unclassified but not widely disseminated statements. I will cite only a few.

Four recent reports all recommend major changes in nuclear strategies and drastic reductions in nuclear force levels.

1. The Spring 1993 issue of *Foreign Affairs* carried an article, coauthored by retired chairman of the Joint Chiefs of Staff Admiral William J. Crowe Jr., that concluded that by the year 2000, the United States and Russia could reduce strategic nuclear forces to 1,000–1,500 warheads each. The article was later expanded into a

book, which added, "Nor is 1,000–1,500 the lowest level obtainable by the early 21st Century."[18]

2. In December 1995, a Stimson Center report, signed by four recently retired four-star officers, recommended moving through a series of four steps to the "goal of elimination" of nuclear weapons.[19]

3. The Canberra Commission, which was appointed by Prime Minister Paul Keating of Australia, recommended in 1996 "a program to achieve a world totally free of nuclear weapons."[20] The Commission members included, among others, Michel Rocard, the former prime minister of France; Joseph Rotblat, the 1995 Nobel Peace Prize winner and one of the designers of the original nuclear bomb; Field Marshal Lord Carver, former chief of the British Defence Staff; General Lee Butler, former commander of the U.S. Strategic Air Command; and myself. The Commission's recommendations were unanimous. They were presented without any qualification or even the slightest note of dissent.

4. A National Academy of Sciences report (1997) stated that reductions by the United States and Russia, within a few years, to a level of 2,000 warheads each "should be easily accommodated within the existing and anticipated strategic force structures of both sides." It then recommended moving to 1,000 warheads each and later to "roughly 300 each."[21]

These four reports should not have come as surprises. For nearly twenty years, more and more Western military and civilian security experts have expressed doubts about the military utility of nuclear weapons. This is what they have said:

1. By 1982, five of the seven retired chiefs of the British Defence Staff expressed their belief that initiating the use of nuclear weapons, in accordance with NATO policy, would lead to disaster. Lord Louis Mountbatten, Chief of Staff from 1959 to 1965, said a few months before he was murdered in 1979: "As a military man I can see no use for any nuclear weapons." And Field Marshal Lord Carver, Chief of Staff from 1973 to 1976, wrote in 1982 that he was

totally opposed to NATO's ever initiating the use of nuclear weapons.[22]

2. Henry Kissinger, speaking in Brussels in 1979, made quite clear he believed that the United States would never initiate a nuclear strike against the Soviet Union, no matter what the provocations. "Our European allies," he said, "should not keep asking us to multiply strategic assurances that we cannot possibly mean or if we do mean, we should not execute because if we execute we risk the destruction of civilization."[23]

3. Melvin Laird, President Nixon's first Secretary of Defense, was reported in the *Washington Post* of April 12, 1982, as saying: "A worldwide zero nuclear option with adequate verification should now be our goal. . . . These weapons . . . are useless for military purposes."

4. Former West German chancellor Helmut Schmidt stated in a 1987 BBC interview: "Flexible response [NATO's strategy calling for the use of nuclear weapons in response to a Warsaw Pact attack by nonnuclear forces] is nonsense. Not out of date, but nonsense. . . . The Western idea, which was created in the 1950s, that we should be willing to use nuclear weapons first, in order to make up for our so-called conventional deficiency, has never convinced me."[24]

5. General Larry Welch, former U.S. Air Force Chief of Staff and previously commander of the Strategic Air Command, recently put the same thought in these words: "Nuclear deterrence depended on someone believing that you would commit an act totally irrational if done."[25]

6. In July 1994, General Charles A. Horner, then chief of the U.S. Space Command, stated: "The nuclear weapon is obsolete. I want to get rid of them all."[26]

7. On December 5, 1996, nineteen senior retired U.S. military officers and forty-two senior admirals and generals from other nations across the world stated their support for the complete elimination of nuclear weapons.

8. On February 2, 1998, 119 present and former heads of state and other senior civilian leaders—including, for example, Helmut Schmidt, Michel Rocard, James Callaghan, Jimmy Carter, and six former prime ministers of Japan—endorsed a similar statement.

In the early 1960s, I had reached conclusions similar to those I have cited. In long private conversations, first with President Kennedy and then with President Johnson, I had recommended, without qualification, that they never initiate, under any circumstances, the use of nuclear weapons.[27] I believe they accepted my recommendations. But neither they nor I could discuss our positions publicly because they were totally contrary to established NATO policy.

In truth, for over thirty years, with respect to our stated nuclear policy, it might be said that "the emperor had no clothes." I do not believe that after 1960, by which time the Soviets had acquired a survivable retaliatory force, any one of our presidents—Eisenhower, Kennedy, Johnson, Nixon, Ford, Carter, Reagan, Bush, or Clinton—would ever have initiated the use of nuclear weapons. Nor would our allies have wished them to do so. To initiate a nuclear strike against a comparably equipped opponent would have been tantamount to committing suicide. To initiate use against a nonnuclear opponent would have been militarily unnecessary, politically indefensible, and morally repugnant.

It was the acceptance of that judgment that led the Canberra Commission to recommend the complete elimination of nuclear weapons. But the Commission went further. It accepted the evidence that the current nuclear posture of both Russia and the United States poses a totally unacceptable danger to the two countries and indeed to the peace of the world. A report by Bruce G. Blair of the Brookings Institution graphically describes the danger.[28] Blair states that both the United States and Russia keep thousands of nuclear warheads on "hair trigger" alert, poised for launch before the opposing side's missiles reach their targets. The "launch on warning" doctrine requires that in less than fifteen minutes a missile attack be detected and analyzed, the decision to retaliate made, and orders to do so disseminated to hundreds of weapons sites. The risk of accidental, inadvertent, or unauthorized launch would exist under the best of conditions. But today, according to Russia's own commanders, their country's alert position is particularly vulnerable. Their command posts will not survive attack, much of their early-warning network is not functioning, safeguards against unauthorized use of nuclear forces are ineffective, large numbers of both their land-based and sea-based forces are inoperative, and the majority of the remainder would not survive a counterforce attack by the United States. The situation is, in Blair's words, "extremely dangerous." Both the United States and Russia, while seeking to deter a vanishing risk of deliberate nuclear aggression, are running a growing risk of stumbling into an inadvertent nuclear war.

The Canberra Commission came to the same conclusion. Therefore, with the strong support of its two military chiefs (Field Marshal Lord Carver and General Lee Butler), it urged that the five declared nuclear powers—China, Russia, Britain, France, and the United States—not only state their unequivocal political commitment to the elimination of nuclear weapons, but accompany that commitment with three immediate steps consistent with fulfilling it:

1. The removal of all nuclear weapons from alert status.
2. The separation of all nuclear warheads from their launch vehicles.
3. A declaration of "no first use" of nuclear weapons against nuclear states, and "no use" against nonnuclear nations.

Years will pass before the Commission's recommendations are fully implemented. But we are beginning to break out of the mind-set that has guided the strategy of the nuclear powers for over four decades. More and more political and military leaders are coming to understand two fundamental truths:

1. We can indeed "put the genie back in the bottle."
2. If we do not, there is a substantial and unacceptable risk that the twenty-first century will witness a nuclear holocaust.

In sum, with the end of the Cold War, if we act to establish a system of collective security, and if we take steps to return to a non-nuclear world, the twenty-first century, while it certainly will not be a century of tranquillity, need not witness the killing, by war, of another 160 (or even 300) million people. Surely that must be not only our hope, not only our dream, but our steadfast objective. I know that some—perhaps many—may consider such a statement so naive, so simplistic, and so idealistic as to be quixotic. But as human beings, citizens with power to influence events in the world, can we be at peace with ourselves if we strive for less? I think not. I hope you will agree.

Notes

Introduction

1. Morley Safer, *Flashbacks: On Returning to Vietnam* (New York, 1990), xix.

2. Remarks of Ambassador Pete Peterson, June 20, 1997, at the conference "Missed Opportunities? Revisiting the Decisions of the Vietnam War, 1945–1965," Hanoi, June 20–23, 1997.

3. H. R. McMaster, *Dereliction of Duty: Lyndon Johnson, Robert McNamara, the Joint Chiefs of Staff, and the Lies That Led to Vietnam* (New York, 1997); Kai Bird, *The Color of Truth: McGeorge Bundy and William Bundy: Brothers in Arms* (New York, 1998); William Bundy, *A Tangled Web: The Making of Foreign Policy in the Nixon Presidency* (New York, 1998); Lewis Sorley, *A Better War: The Unexamined Victories and Final Tragedy of America's Last Years in Vietnam* (New York, 1999).

4. Quoted in ABC News, *Day One,* January 10, 1994, "They Were Young and Brave."

5. Quoted in Neil Sheehan, *After the War Was Over: Hanoi and Saigon* (New York, 1991), 47.

6. Robert S. McNamara with Brian VanDeMark, *In Retrospect: The Tragedy and Lessons of Vietnam* (New York, 1995), xv, xvi, xviii; McNamara, *Argument Without End: In Search of Answers to the Vietnam Tragedy* (New York, 1999).

7. McNamara, *In Retrospect,* xviii.

1. The Vietnam War and the Transformation of America

I am grateful to Louis Galambos, George C. Herring, and James T. Patterson for their comments on an earlier draft of this essay.

1. Important books on the legacy of the war include George K. Osborn, Asa A. Clark IV, Daniel J. Kaufman, and Douglas E. Lute, eds., *Democracy, Strategy, and Vietnam: Implications for American Policymaking* (Lexington, Mass., 1987); D. Michael Shafer, ed., *The Legacy: The Vietnam War in the American Imagination* (Boston, 1990); John Carlos Rowe and Rick Berg, eds., *The Vietnam War and American Culture* (New York, 1991); and William Head and Lawrence E. Grinter, eds., *Looking Back on the Vietnam War: A 1990s Perspective on the Decisions, Combat, and Legacies* (Westport, Conn., 1993). Arnold R. Isaacs, *Vietnam Shadows: The War, Its Ghosts, and Its Legacy* (Baltimore, 1997), is a superb analysis of the impact of the war on various aspects of American life.

2. Walter H. Capps, *The Unfinished War: Vietnam and the American Conscience,* 2d ed. (Boston, 1990), ix–xi; Isaacs, *Vietnam Shadows,* ix.

3. Two impressive accounts of veterans who returned are William Broyles Jr., *Brothers in Arms: A Journey from War to Peace* (New York, 1986); and Frederick Downs, *No Longer Enemies, Not Yet Friends: An American Soldier Returns to Vietnam* (New York, 1991).

4. In *A Tangled Web: The Making of Foreign Policy in the Nixon Presidency* (New York, 1998), William Bundy, who served in the Defense and State Departments from 1961 to 1969, offers a sharp critique of the diplomacy of Richard Nixon and Henry Kissinger. In a long letter challenging Tony Judt's review in the *New York Review of Books,* former Secretary of State Kissinger complains: "It is a pity that the wounds of Vietnam are never permitted to close. It is especially sad when they are being ripped open by someone [William Bundy] who had himself been subjected, in and out of office, to the kind of personal assault he has now visited on his successors." *New York Review of Books,* September 24, 1998, 80.

5. See George Bush and Brent Scowcroft, *A World Transformed* (New York, 1998), 354, 431, 466, 483–84, 486–87; Herbert S. Parmet, *George Bush: The Life of a Lone Star Yankee* (New York, 1997), 58–59, 477–82, 500–508; and David Maraniss, *First in His Class: The Biography of Bill Clinton* (New York, 1995), 85–88, 105–6, 178–82, 198–205, which traces Clinton's tangled relationship with the Vietnam War. Dole accentuated the differences between himself and Clinton in his speech accepting the Republican nomination. After reminding his audience that he was born in 1923, he proclaimed: "Let me be the bridge to an America that only the unknowing call myth. Let me be the bridge to a time of tranquility, faith, and confi-

dence in action. To those who say it was never so, that America has not been better, I say, you're wrong, and, I know, because I was there. I have seen it. I remember." *New York Times,* August 16, 1996.

6. Robert S. McNamara with Brian VanDeMark, *In Retrospect: The Tragedy and Lessons of Vietnam* (New York, 1995), xi–xviii, 319–35. The *New York Times* editorial of April 12, 1995, along with other reactions to the book, is reprinted in an appendix to the Vintage Books edition, published in 1996. For other reactions to *In Retrospect,* see Paul Hendrickson, *The Living and the Dead: Robert McNamara and Five Lives of a Lost War* (New York, 1996), 376–80; and Kai Bird, *The Color of Truth: McGeorge Bundy and William Bundy: Brothers in Arms* (New York, 1998), 396–409, which analyzes the efforts of the Bundy brothers to deal with the legacy of the war.

7. On movies dealing with the Vietnam War, see the essays in Linda Dittmar and Gene Michaud, eds., *From Hanoi to Hollywood: The Vietnam War in American Film* (New Brunswick, N.J., 1990); and Caryn James, "Complex Warriors and Victims," *New York Times,* May 29, 1998.

8. H. Bruce Franklin, *M.I.A., or, Mythmaking in America* (New Brunswick, N.J., 1993), 3–35.

9. James Reston Jr., *Sherman's March and Vietnam* (New York, 1984), 5.

10. Richard A. Melanson, *American Foreign Policy since the Vietnam War: The Search for Consensus from Nixon to Clinton* (New York, 1996), 3–37, analyzes the impact of the Vietnam War on the Cold War consensus, while the essays in Osborn, Clark, Kaufman, and Lute, *Democracy, Strategy, and Vietnam,* offer more specialized assessments of the war's impact.

11. Lou Cannon, *President Reagan: The Role of a Lifetime* (New York, 1991), 281–82, 316–17, 334–39; H. W. Brands, *The Devil We Knew: Americans and the Cold War* (New York, 1993), 164–65.

12. I. M. Destler, Leslie H. Gelb, and Anthony Lake, *Our Own Worst Enemy: The Unmaking of American Foreign Policy* (New York, 1984), 91–126.

13. Robert Dallek, *Flawed Giant: Lyndon Johnson and His Times, 1961–1973* (New York, 1998), 272–73, 350, 511–12; Acheson quoted in Walter Isaacson and Evan Thomas, *The Wise Men: Six Friends and the World They Made: Acheson, Bohlen, Harriman, Kennan, Lovett, McCloy* (New York, 1986), 693–703.

14. Quoted in William C. Berman, *William Fulbright and the Vietnam War: The Dissent of a Political Realist* (Kent, Ohio, 1988), 64.

15. Thomas E. Mann, "Making Foreign Policy: President and Con-

gress," in Mann, ed., *A Question of Balance: The President, Congress, and Foreign Policy* (Washington, D.C., 1990), 1–34. A different view is advanced in Barbara Hinckley, *Less Than Meets the Eye: Foreign Policy Making and the Myth of the Assertive Congress* (Chicago, 1994), 1–22.

16. Loch K. Johnson, *America's Secret Power: The CIA in a Democratic Society* (New York, 1989), 207–33.

17. John Ranelagh, *The Agency: The Rise and Decline of the CIA* (New York, 1986), 584–626.

18. Quoted in Lloyd C. Gardner, *Approaching Vietnam: From World War II through Dienbienphu, 1941–1954* (New York, 1988), 196–97.

19. Phillip B. Davidson, *Vietnam at War: The History, 1946–1975* (New York, 1988), 795.

20. Isaacs, *Vietnam Shadows,* x.

21. Michael C. C. Adams, *The Best War Ever: America and World War II* (Baltimore, 1994), 1–19, 69–90, 136–59.

22. Philip Roth, *American Pastoral* (Boston, 1997), 40–41.

23. James T. Patterson, *Grand Expectations: The United States, 1945–1974* (New York, 1996), vii–ix, 61–81, 105–36.

24. Michael Kammen's essay "The Problem of American Exceptionalism: A Reconsideration," in *In the Past Lane: Historical Perspectives on American Culture* (New York, 1997), 169–98, offers an intelligent summary of the extensive historical literature on the extent of America's distinctiveness as a nation. The essays in Bryon E. Shafer, ed., *Is America Different? A New Look at American Exceptionalism* (Oxford, 1991), are also helpful, as is H. W. Brands, *What America Owes the World: The Struggle for the Soul of Foreign Policy* (New York, 1998).

25. Winthrop quoted in Loren Baritz, *Backfire: A History of How American Culture Led Us into Vietnam and Made Us Fight the Way We Did* (New York, 1985), 26; Anders Stephanson, *Manifest Destiny: American Expansionism and the Empire of Right* (New York, 1995), 4–27.

26. Richard Slotkin, *Gunfighter Nation: The Myth of the Frontier in Twentieth-Century America* (New York, 1992), 14.

27. Arthur M. Schlesinger Jr., "The Theory of America: Experiment or Destiny?" in *The Cycles of American History* (Boston, 1986), 6–12.

28. Quoted in Walter A. McDougall, *Promised Land, Crusader State: The American Encounter with the World since 1776* (Boston, 1997), 36.

29. Schlesinger, *The Cycles of American History,* 14–19; McDougall, *Promised Land, Crusader State,* 76–212.

30. Josiah Strong, *Our Country,* ed. Jurgen Herbst (Cambridge, Mass., 1963), 214–17.

31. Schlesinger, *The Cycles of American History,* 20; McDougall, *Promised Land, Crusader State,* 122–98.

32. Truman quoted in McDougall, *Promised Land, Crusader State,* 169; Reagan quoted in Schlesinger, *The Cycles of American History,* 16.

33. Tom Engelhardt, *The End of Victory Culture: Cold War America and the Disillusioning of a Generation* (New York, 1995), 3–53.

34. John W. Dower, *War without Mercy: Race and Power in the Pacific War* (New York, 1986), 3–180.

35. Engelhardt, *The End of Victory Culture,* 54–171; Warren I. Cohen, *America's Response to China: A History of Sino-American Relations,* 3d ed. (New York, 1990), 162–84.

36. John Lewis Gaddis, *Strategies of Containment: A Critical Appraisal of Postwar American National Security Policy* (New York, 1982), 198–236.

37. Quoted in Theodore C. Sorensen, *Kennedy* (New York, 1965), 246–48.

38. James N. Giglio, *The Presidency of John F. Kennedy* (Lawrence, Kans., 1991), 45–96, 123–58.

39. Slotkin, *Gunfighter Nation,* 489–533.

40. Quoted in Sheehan, *A Bright Shining Lie,* 58.

41. George C. Herring, *America's Longest War: The United States and Vietnam, 1950–1975,* 3d ed. (New York, 1996), 81–119, provides an excellent account of these debates.

42. John Hellmann, *American Myth and the Legacy of Vietnam* (New York, 1986), 51, 53–69.

43. Philip Caputo, *A Rumor of War* (New York, 1977), xii.

44. Baritz, *Backfire,* 57–143; McNamara quoted in Deborah Shapley, *Promise and Power: The Life and Times of Robert McNamara* (Boston, 1993), 51.

45. George C. Herring, *LBJ and Vietnam: A Different Kind of War* (Austin, Tex., 1994), 35.

46. Sheehan, *A Bright Shining Lie,* 285, 287–305. H. R. McMaster, *Dereliction of Duty: Lyndon Johnson, Robert McNamara, the Joint Chiefs of Staff,*

and the Lies That Led to Vietnam (New York, 1997), analyzes the complex position of the Joint Chiefs of Staff from 1961 through July 1965.

47. Christian G. Appy, *Working-Class War: American Combat Soldiers and Vietnam* (Chapel Hill, N.C., 1993), 57–62; Slotkin, *Gunfighter Nation,* 512–13; Garry Wills, *John Wayne's America* (New York, 1997), 27.

48. Ron Kovic, *Born on the Fourth of July* (New York, 1976), 43–45, 60–61.

49. James Carroll, *An American Requiem: God, My Father, and the War That Came Between Us* (Boston, 1996), 15, 30–33.

50. David E. James, "Documenting the Vietnam War," in Dittmar and Michaud, *From Hanoi to Hollywood,* 244–45; Engelhardt, *The End of Victory Culture,* 11–14.

51. Engelhardt, *The End of Victory Culture,* 14.

52. Michael Lee Lanning and Dan Cragg, *Inside the VC and the NVA: The Real Story of North Vietnam's Armed Forces* (New York, 1992), 16–190; Otto J. Lehrack, *No Shining Armor: The Marines at War in Vietnam, an Oral History* (Lawrence, Kans., 1992), 99–304.

53. Lanning and Cragg, *Inside the VC and the NVA,* 215–36; Broyles, *Brothers in Arms,* 3.

54. Engelhardt, *The End of Victory Culture,* 202–3.

55. Hellmann, *American Myth,* 74.

56. Ibid., 78–95.

57. Bui Diem with David Chanoff, *In the Jaws of History* (Boston, 1987), 106–215.

58. Bundy quoted in McNamara, *In Retrospect,* 186; Rusk quoted in Anne E. Blair, *Lodge in Vietnam: A Patriot Abroad* (New Haven, Conn., 1995), 138.

59. *Fortunate Son: The Autobiography of Lewis B. Puller, Jr.* (New York, 1991), 132–35; Robert Mason, *Chickenhawk* (New York, 1983), 224–26, 403–4.

60. Sheehan, *A Bright Shining Lie,* 536–37, 553–58, 567–68.

61. Caputo, *A Rumor of War,* xii.

62. Appy, *Working-Class War,* 117–297; Eric M. Bergerud, *Red Thunder, Tropic Lightning: The World of a Combat Division in Vietnam* (Boulder, Colo., 1993), 9–42, 89–194.

63. Lt. Gen. Harold G. Moore and Joseph L. Galloway, *We Were Soldiers*

Once . . . and Young: Ia Drang: The Battle That Changed the War in Vietnam (New York, 1992), 342–43.

64. Mason, *Chickenhawk,* 162; Broyles, *Brothers in Arms,* 165–66.

65. Samuel Hynes, *The Soldiers' Tale: Bearing Witness to Modern War* (New York, 1997), 214–15.

66. David Donovan, *Once a Warrior King: Memories of an Officer in Vietnam* (New York, 1985), 324; Tobias Wolff, *In Pharaoh's Army: Memories of the Lost War* (New York, 1994), 23.

67. Appy, *Working-Class War,* 162–73, 190–205.

68. Donovan, *Once a Warrior King,* 28, 33; Abrams quoted in Lewis Sorley, *Thunderbolt: General Creighton Abrams and the Army of His Times* (New York, 1992), 353.

69. Morley Safer, *Flashbacks: On Returning to Vietnam* (New York, 1990), 137–52; Engelhardt, *The End of Victory Culture,* 187–93.

70. Michael Bilton and Kevin Sim, *Four Hours in My Lai* (New York, 1992), 1–46; David L. Anderson, ed., *Facing My Lai: Moving beyond the Massacre* (Lawrence, Kans., 1998), 1–17; Engelhardt, *The End of Victory Culture,* 215–27.

71. Kennedy quoted in Arthur M. Schlesinger Jr., *Robert Kennedy and His Times* (Boston, 1978), 2:860; Westmoreland quoted in Samuel Zaffiri, *Westmoreland: A Biography of General William C. Westmoreland* (New York, 1994), 245–46.

72. Robert D. Schulzinger, *A Time for War: The United States and Vietnam, 1941–1975* (New York, 1997), 261–63, 274–304; Joan Hoff, *Nixon Reconsidered* (New York, 1994), 208–42.

73. Olivier Todd, *Cruel April: The Fall of Saigon,* trans. Stephen Becker (New York, 1990), 346–411.

74. J. William Fulbright, *The Crippled Giant: American Foreign Policy and Its Domestic Consequences* (New York, 1972), 177–279.

75. George F. Kennan, *The Cloud of Danger: Current Realities of American Foreign Policy* (Boston, 1977), 4–5.

76. Norman Podhoretz, *Why We Were in Vietnam* (New York, 1982), 133–210.

77. Cannon, *President Reagan,* 109, 162–63, 296–97; Reagan quoted in Reston, *Sherman's March and Vietnam,* 263–64.

78. Admiral U.S. Grant Sharp, *Strategy for Defeat: Vietnam in Retrospect*

(Novato, Calif., 1978), 267–71; William C. Westmoreland, *A Soldier Reports* (New York, 1976), 542.

79. William Colby, *Lost Victory: A Firsthand Account of America's Sixteen-Year Involvement in Vietnam* (Chicago, 1989), 6.

80. Kovic, *Born on the Fourth of July,* 98; Puller, *Fortunate Son,* 260.

81. Myra MacPherson, *Long Time Passing: Vietnam and the Haunted Generation* (New York, 1984), 3–8, 713–33. Eric T. Dean Jr., *Shook over Hell: Post-Traumatic Stress, Vietnam, and the Civil War* (Cambridge, Mass., 1997), is a fascinating comparison of the psychological problems of Civil War and Vietnam veterans.

82. Hellmann, *American Myth,* x.

83. Isaacs, *Vietnam Shadows,* 136.

84. Patterson, *Grand Expectations,* 782.

85. Ronald Steel, "Who Is Us?" *The New Republic,* September 14 and 21, 1998, 13–14; Vincent Canby, "Saving a Nation's Pride of Being," *New York Times,* August 10, 1998.

86. Robert D. Kaplan, *An Empire Wilderness: Travels into America's Future* (New York, 1998), 3–20, 341–53.

2. From Metaphor to Quagmire

The author would like to thank Ed Ayers, Lisa Cobbs, Lou Galambos, Dan Geary, Steve Innes, Peter Kastor, Mel Leffler, Nelson Lichtenstein, Charles McCurdy, Charles Neu, Doug Rossinow, Bruce Schulman, Anders Stephanson, and Nancy Trotic for their comments on earlier drafts of this essay.

1. On Vietnam as tragedy, see David W. Levy, *The Debate over Vietnam* (Baltimore, 1995), 177. On other characterizations of the war, see Terry H. Anderson, *The Movement and the Sixties* (New York, 1995), 417; Lloyd Gardner, "America's War in Vietnam," in D. Michael Shafer, ed., *The Legacy: The Vietnam War in the American Imagination* (Boston, 1990), 9; Barbara Tischler, "Promise and Paradox: The 1960s and American Optimism," in Shafer, *Legacy,* 30; Peter B. Levy, "Blacks and the Vietnam War," in Shafer, *Legacy,* 215; Peter McInerney, "Apocalypse Then: Hollywood Looks at Vietnam," *Film Quarterly* 33, no. 2 (Winter 1979–80): 22; David Broder, quoted in Michael S. Sherry, *In the Shadow of War: The United States since the 1930s* (New Haven, Conn., 1995), 336; and James T. Pat-

terson, *Grand Expectations: The United States, 1945–1974* (New York, 1996), 769. On forgetting the war, see Sherry, *Shadow of War,* 335; Anderson, *Movement,* 475; Andrew Martin, *Receptions of War: Vietnam in American Culture* (Norman, Okla., 1993), 10; and Loren Baritz, *Backfire: A History of How American Culture Led Us into Vietnam and Made Us Fight the Way We Did* (New York, 1985), 11. George Herring, "The Meaning of Vietnam," in Robert Griffeth, ed. *Major Problems in American History since 1945* (Lexington, Mass., 1992), 438. Ford is quoted in Albert Auster and Leonard Quart, *How the War Was Remembered: Hollywood and Vietnam* (New York, 1988), 131. On forgetting vets, see Levy, *Debate over Vietnam,* 178. Veteran is quoted in Richard Moser, "Talkin' the Vietnam Blues: Vietnam Oral History and Our Popular Memory of War," in Shafer, *Legacy,* 108.

2. "Haunt us" quotation is from Myra MacPherson, in Bill McCloud, *What Should We Tell Our Children about Vietnam?* (Norman, Okla., 1989), 88. See also Marilyn B. Young, *The Vietnam Wars: 1945–1990* (New York, 1991), 328; and E. J. Dionne, *Why Americans Hate Politics* (New York, 1991), 12, 332. For a summary of the debate over the military failure, see James S. Olson and Randy Roberts, *Where the Domino Fell: America and Vietnam, 1945 to 1990* (New York, 1991), 271–72; and Norman Podhoretz, *Why We Were in Vietnam* (New York, 1982). Peter Boyer, "Is It Prime Time for Vietnam?" *New York Times,* August 2, 1987, quoted in Martin, *Receptions of War,* 3. "It don't mean nothin' " quotation and analysis of this metaphor are from Richard A. Sullivan, "The War in American Fiction, Poetry, and Drama," in Shafer, *Legacy,* 157.

3. Numbers killed are from Michael H. Hunt, *Lyndon Johnson's War: America's Cold War Crusade in Vietnam, 1945–1968* (New York, 1996), 123, 125. Estimates of those killed and wounded over the course of the entire war are far higher. Robert Schulzinger, in *A Time for War: The United States and Vietnam, 1941–1975* (New York, 1997), 335, puts the number of people who died over the course of the war at 3 million. Baritz, citing a report of the Senate Subcommittee on Refugees, estimates that 2 million Vietnamese were killed and 4.5 million wounded (*Backfire,* 344). For age of Americans killed, see Young, *Vietnam Wars,* 319. For number of disabilities, see D. Michael Shafer, "The Vietnam Combat Experience: The Human Legacy," in Shafer, *Legacy,* 80. For number of orphans, see Hunt, *Lyndon Johnson's War,* 123.

4. Hunt, *Lyndon Johnson's War,* 123; Schulzinger, *A Time for War,* 335; Pamela Constable, "After Suffering Vietnam, Amerasians Still Suffering," *Washington Post,* April 13, 1998.

5. Young, *Vietnam Wars,* 319. On returning vets, see Herring, "Meaning of Vietnam," 434; and Ellen Frey-Wouters and Robert S. Laufer, *Legacy of a War: The American Soldier in Vietnam* (Armonk, N.Y., 1986). On wounded veterans, see Leonard Quart and Albert Auster, "The Wounded Vet in Postwar Film," *Social Policy* 13, no. 2 (Fall 1982): 24–31.

6. On spiritual legacy, see Herring, "Meaning of Vietnam," 438. On invincibility, see Anderson, *Movement,* 417; Bruce Taylor, "The Vietnam War Movie," in Shafer, *Legacy,* 204; Jimmy Carter, "Profound Moral Crisis," in Robert J. McMahon, ed., *Major Problems in the History of the Vietnam War* (Lexington, Mass., 1995), 609; and Marilyn B. Young, "The Vietnam War in American Memory," in Marvin E. Gettleman, Jane Franklin, Marilyn B. Young, and H. Bruce Franklin, eds., *Vietnam and America: A Documented History* (New York, 1995), 516. On omnipotence, see Arthur Miller, "The Lessons of Denial," in Harrison E. Salisbury, ed., *Vietnam Reconsidered: Lessons from a War* (New York, 1984), 313. Robert S. McNamara, *In Retrospect: The Tragedy and Lessons of Vietnam* (New York, 1996), 323. On humility, see Podhoretz, *Why We Were in Vietnam,* 12. Hoffmann is quoted in Paul S. Boyer, *Promises to Keep: The United States since World War II* (Lexington, Mass., 1995), 352.

7. Boyer, *Promises to Keep.* Grass is quoted in Podhoretz, *Why We Were in Vietnam,* 15. On the war as crime, see Young, "Vietnam War in American Memory," 516; Podhoretz, *Why We Were in Vietnam,* 14; and H. R. McMaster, *Dereliction of Duty: Lyndon Johnson, Robert McNamara, the Joint Chiefs of Staff, and the Lies That Led to Vietnam* (New York, 1997).

8. On exceptionalism, see Lloyd Gardner, "America's War in Vietnam: The End of Exceptionalism?" in Shafer, *Legacy,* 10–12. On late-nineteenth-century concerns about the demise of exceptionalism, see Dorothy Ross, *The Origins of American Social Science* (New York, 1991); and Martin Burke, *The Conundrum of Class: Public Discourse on the Social Order in America* (Chicago, 1995). Taylor interview is in Michael Charlton and Anthony Moncrieff, *Many Reasons Why: The American Involvement in Vietnam* (New York, 1978), 239–40, quoted in Gardner, "America's War in Vietnam," 28. On reshaping the world, see Gardner, "America's War in Vietnam," 28; and Hunt, *Lyndon Johnson's War,* 128. George W. Ball, "The Les-

sons of Vietnam: Have We Learned or Only Failed?" *New York Times Sunday Magazine,* April 1, 1973, 52.

9. On "No more Vietnams," see Sherry, *Shadow of War,* 335. Poll data are cited in Herring, "Meaning of Vietnam," 439. On the "Vietnam syndrome," see Martin, *Receptions of War,* 5; Young, "Vietnam War in American Memory," 520; Levy, *Debate over Vietnam,* 171, 174; Podhoretz, *Why We Were in Vietnam,* 12; Patterson, *Grand Expectations,* 769; and Boyer, *Promises to Keep,* 352.

10. On the new basis for intervention, see Sherry, *Shadow of War,* 336; Walter Goldstein, "The Lessons of the Vietnam War," *Bulletin of the Atomic Scientists* 26, no. 2 (February 1970): 41; Levy, *Debate over Vietnam,* 170–72; McNamara, *In Retrospect,* 330; Ball, "Lessons of Vietnam," 47; Jeremy M. Devine, *Vietnam at 24 Frames a Second* (Jefferson, N.C., 1995), 334; Ronald Reagan, "A Noble and Just Cause," in McMahon, *Major Problems,* 615; and Hunt, *Lyndon Johnson's War,* 27. On limiting the press, see Goldstein, "Lessons of the Vietnam War," 41; and Hunt, *Lyndon Johnson's War,* 127. On other interventions, see Hunt, *Lyndon Johnson's War,* 126–27. Bush is quoted in Young, "Vietnam War in American Memory," 521.

11. For the Civil War comparison, see Richard Holbrooke in McCloud, *What Should We Tell Our Children?* and Young, "Vietnam War in American Memory," 516. On divisions that the war created, see Sol W. Sanders and William Henderson, "The Consequences of Vietnam," *Orbis* 21, no. 1 (Spring 1977): 61; William Sullivan, "Positive Consequences," in McMahon, *Major Problems,* 612; and McNamara, *In Retrospect,* 319, 322–23. Bush is quoted in Young, "Vietnam War in American Memory," 520. Charles E. Neu, "Robert McNamara's Journey to Hanoi: Reflections on a Lost War," *Reviews in American History* 25 (1997): 729.

12. For an insightful summary of these points, see Goldstein, "Lessons of the Vietnam War," 43–45. For a similar perspective, see Schulzinger, *A Time for War,* 335–36.

13. On Williams, see Doug Rossinow, "Restless Natives," *Reviews in American History* 25 (1997): 163–73. On the New Left in general, see Rossinow, *The Politics of Authenticity: Liberalism, Christianity, and the New Left in America* (New York, 1998); Peter Novick, *That Noble Dream: The "Objectivity Question" and the American Historical Profession* (New York, 1988), chap. 13; and James Miller, *Democracy Is in the Streets: From Port Huron to the Siege of Chicago* (New York, 1987).

14. On Vietnam's contribution to the imperial presidency, see Patterson, *Grand Expectations,* 769; and Boyer, *Promises to Keep,* 352. Sherry, *Shadow of War,* 332. On secrecy, see Anderson, *Movement,* 163; and George S. McGovern, "America in Vietnam," in Patrick J. Hearden, ed., *Vietnam: Four American Perspectives* (West Lafayette, Ind., 1990), 23.

15. On the resurgence of Congress, see James L. Sundquist, *The Decline and Resurgence of Congress* (Washington, D.C., 1981). Sidney M. Milkis, *The President and the Parties: The Transformation of the American Party System since the New Deal* (New York, 1993), 240.

16. Seymour Hersh in McCloud, *What Should We Tell Our Children?* 61.

17. On distrust, see Anderson, *Movement,* 418; and Schulzinger, *A Time for War,* 335. Veterans Administration quotation is from Young, *Vietnam Wars,* 321. Patterson, *Grand Expectations,* 769. On the ideological range of public distrust, see Leo Cawley, "Refighting the War: Why the Movies Are in Vietnam," *Village Voice,* September 8, 1987, 20.

18. McGovern, "America in Vietnam"; Sherry, *Shadow of War,* 333.

19. On the McGovernite rift in the Democratic party, see Levy, "Blacks and the Vietnam War," 210. Dionne, *Why Americans Hate Politics,* 51–52. On the condition of the Democratic party, see Dionne, *Why Americans Hate Politics,* 125–26; McGovern, "America in Vietnam," 24; and Michael X. Delli Carpini, "Vietnam, Ideology, and Domestic Politics," in Shafer, *Legacy,* 322.

20. Johnson is quoted in William H. Chafe, *The Unfinished Journey: America since World War II* (New York, 1995), 300. On the economy, see Chafe, *Unfinished Journey,* 301, 341; McGovern, "America in Vietnam," 23; and Levy, "Blacks and the Vietnam War," 210. On trade deficits, see Akira Iriye, foreword to Hearden, *Vietnam,* vii; Gardner, "America's War in Vietnam," 10; Hunt, *Lyndon Johnson's War,* 125; and Schulzinger, *A Time for War,* 335.

Besides those discussed in the text, there are many other legacies of Vietnam, ranging from the war's impact on the media to the domestication of violence. Regarding the former, most analysts agree that television news coverage came of age with Vietnam. Edward Fouhy, "The Effect of the Vietnam War on Broadcast Journalism," in Salisbury, *Vietnam Reconsidered,* 89–90. It was Vietnam that demonstrated to broadcasters and viewers alike that the visual image could be as powerful as the written word. Barbara Tischler, "Counterculture and Over-the-Counter Culture," in Shafer, *Leg-*

acy, 283. The episodic impact of television coverage of milestones such as President Kennedy's funeral or civil rights protests was regularized in the steady stream of images coming from Vietnam. As for violence, even cultural artifacts ostensibly far removed from Vietnam, such as the films *Bonnie and Clyde* and *Taxi Driver,* were drenched in blood attributed ultimately to the war. Michael Anderegg, ed., *Inventing Vietnam: The War in Film and Television* (Philadelphia, 1991), 15; Olson and Roberts, *Where the Domino Fell,* 265–66; Levy, *Debate over Vietnam,* 175. Vietnam also contributed to the backlash against science and technology. See Goldstein, "Lessons of the Vietnam War," 322.

21. On changes in American culture, see Martin, *Receptions of War,* 19. John Hellmann, *American Myth and the Legacy of Vietnam* (New York, 1986), x.

22. On the Mall memorial, see John Bodnar, *Remaking America: Public Memory, Commemoration, and Patriotism in the Twentieth Century* (Princeton, N.J., 1992), 5. Young, *Vietnam Wars,* 328. On the New York memorial, see Michael Clark, "Remembering Vietnam," *Cultural Critique* 3 (1986): 69, 74. Tom Engelhardt, *The End of Victory Culture: Cold War America and the Disillusioning of a Generation* (New York, 1995), 1–15; on Vietnam as the "graveyard" of victory culture, see p. 10. On this point, see also Hellmann, *American Myth,* 4.

23. On the Munich metaphor, see Hunt, *Lyndon Johnson's War,* 125; and Sherry, *Shadow of War,* 286. On the domestic component of the Vietnam metaphor, see, for example, Schulzinger, *A Time for War,* 329; and Shafer, *Legacy,* vii. Podhoretz, *Why We Were in Vietnam,* 10. Richard Sullivan, "Recreation of Vietnam," in Shafer, *Legacy,* 176. On Vietnam as a "site of struggle," see Martin, *Receptions of War,* 4. Martin draws upon Michel Foucault, claiming that Vietnam is a "node within a network" of discourses. See Michel Foucault, *The Archaeology of Knowledge* (New York, 1972), 23.

24. On the evolution of policy-based careers, see Milkis, *The President and the Parties,* chap. 9. On military prestige, see Charles C. Moskos and John Sibley Butler, *All That We Can Be: Black Leadership and Racial Integration the Army Way* (New York, 1996), 33. On the metaphorical use of vets, see Moser, "Talkin' the Vietnam Blues," 104, 114, 116. On vets as an interest group, see Levy, *Debate over Vietnam,* 178; and Hunt, *Lyndon Johnson's War,* 126.

25. Sherry, *Shadow of War,* x. As JoAnne Brown puts it, metaphorical language establishes the central characteristics of political events by creating assumptions about matters that are not seen. Once accepted, a metaphorical view becomes the organizing conception into which the public thereafter arranges items of news that fit. See JoAnne Brown, *The Definition of a Profession: The Authority of Metaphor in the History of Intelligence Testing, 1890–1930* (Princeton, N.J., 1992), 13–14, 33.

26. Todd Gitlin, *The Sixties: Years of Hope, Days of Rage* (New York, 1987), 179–84; Potter is quoted on p. 180. On symbols and structural problems, see Godfrey Hodgson, *America in Our Time* (New York, 1976), 300.

27. Coppola is quoted in Devine, *Vietnam at 24 Frames a Second,* 185. On the film's arsenal, see McInerney, "Apocalypse Then," 32.

28. Virtually all accounts of the 1960s refer to the decline in authority. For a contemporary commentary on this decline, see Norman Mailer, *The Armies of the Night: History as a Novel, the Novel as History* (New York, 1968). For other commentaries, see Hodgson, *America in Our Time,* 318; Linda Dittmar and Gene Michaud, "America's Vietnam War Films: Marching toward Denial," in Dittmar and Michaud, eds., *From Hanoi to Hollywood: The Vietnam War in American Film* (New Brunswick, N.J., 1990), 7; Tischler, "Promise and Paradox," 30; Tischler, "Counterculture," 281; and W. J. Rorabaugh, "Challenging Authority, Seeking Community, and Empowerment in the New Left, Black Power, and Feminism," in Brian Balogh, ed., *Integrating the Sixties: The Origins, Structures, and Legitimacy of Public Policy in a Turbulent Decade* (University Park, Pa., 1996), 106–43. For polling data, see Gary Orren, "The Fall from Grace: The Public's Loss of Faith in Government," in Joseph S. Nye Jr., Philip D. Zelikow, and David C. King, eds., *Why People Don't Trust Government* (Cambridge, Mass., 1997), 80.

The decline of authority was not limited to government or to the United States. On the international challenge to authority, see Nicholas N. Kittrie, *The War against Authority: From the Crisis of Legitimacy to a New Social Contract* (Baltimore, 1995). Nixon's vice president, Spiro Agnew, referred to the protests against American involvement in Vietnam as a "holy war." For this and other commentaries on social and political divisions, see Sherry, *Shadow of War,* 299. See also Dittmar and Michaud, "America's Vietnam War Films," 5; Henry Kissinger in McCloud, *What Should We Tell Our Children?* 68; and Olson and Roberts, *Where the Domino Fell,* 273. "Destroy the bonds" quotation is from Moser, "Talkin' the Vietnam Blues," 104. On the fragmentation of national identity, see Sherry, *Shadow of War,* 285; Herring, "Meaning of Vietnam," 438; Dittmar and Michaud, "America's Vietnam War Films," 7; Olson and Roberts, *Where the Domino Fell,* 264; and Young, "Vietnam War in American Memory," 516–18.

29. On the nature of Vietnam footage, see Michael X. Delli Carpini, "Vietnam and the Press," in Shafer, *Legacy,* 138.

30. "War that traumatized" quotation is from McInerney, "Apocalypse Then," 22. See also David Everett Whillock, "Narrative Structure in *Apocalypse Now,*" in Owen W. Gilman Jr. and Lorrie Smith, *America Rediscovered: Critical Essays on Literature and Film of the Vietnam War* (New York, 1990), 306. On *The Green Berets,* see McInerney, "Apocalypse Then," 23. On taking politics out of the war, see Whillock, "Narrative Structure," 303. On the sudden interest in Vietnam by filmmakers, see Leo Cawley, "Refighting the War: Why the Movies Are in Vietnam," *Village Voice,* September 8, 1987, 18. For the number of Vietnam films, see Devine, *Vietnam at 24 Frames a Second,* xii.

31. Michael Anderegg, "Hollywood and Vietnam," in Anderegg, *Inventing Vietnam,* 15. See also McInerney, "Apocalypse Then," 23. On the personal anguish of soldiers, see Cawley, "Refighting the War," 20. On the absence of command-level films, see Dittmar and Michaud, "America's Vietnam War Films," 6. On situational loyalty, see J. Hoberman, "Hollywood on the Mekong," *Village Voice,* September 8, 1997, 57.

32. On reconciliation, see McInerney, "Apocalypse Then," 24–27; Devine, *Vietnam at 24 Frames a Second,* 157; and Clark, "Remembering Vietnam," 46–78. Rambo quote is in Devine, *Vietnam at 24 Frames a Second,* 231. Hoberman, "Hollywood on the Mekong," 19, 57. See also Sullivan, "The War in American Fiction," 175.

33. *Time* is quoted in Olson and Roberts, *Where the Domino Fell,* 268. Martin, *Receptions of War,* 22.

34. Anderson, *Movement,* 135. Delli Carpini, "Vietnam, Ideology, and Domestic Politics," 303, 311. Tischler, "Counterculture," 298.

35. On the war and the student movement, see Gitlin, *The Sixties,* 186–89. Chafe, *Unfinished Journey,* 468–69.

36. For a similar view of Vietnam as causal agent, see conclusion to Nye, Zelikow, and King, *Why People Don't Trust Government,* 270–71.

37. On abolishing the quota system for admissions, see Reed Ueda, "The

Progressive State and the Legacy of Collective Immigrant Identities," in Morton Keller and R. Shep Melnick, eds., *Taking Stock: American Government in the Twentieth Century* (Cambridge University Press, forthcoming); see also Patterson, *Grand Expectations,* 577–78. Statistics on recent European immigration are from Patterson, *Grand Expectations,* 578. Peter Skerry, "The Racialization of Immigration Policy," in Keller and Melnick, *Taking Stock,* 131. On Title VII, see Hugh Davis Graham, *The Civil Rights Era: Origins and Development of National Policy, 1960–1972* (New York, 1990), 133–39, chap. 8.

38. And despite America's relative class harmony, class has also proven to be far more divisive than the struggles over Vietnam.

39. See David B. Truman, *The Governmental Process: Political Interests and Public Opinion* (New York, 1951); E. E. Schattschneider, *The Semi-sovereign People* (New York, 1960); and Theodore Lowi, *The End of Liberalism* (New York, 1969). For a brief history of pluralism in the United States, see Charles W. Anderson, "Political Design and the Representation of Interests," in Philippe C. Schmitter and Gerhard Lehmbruch, *Trends towards Corporatist Intermediation* (Beverly Hills, Calif., 1979), 271–74. On the explosion of public interest groups, see David Vogel, *Kindred Strangers: The Uneasy Relationship between Politics and Business in America* (Princeton, N.J., 1996), 153. Vogel correctly points out that many of the procedural reforms demanded by the public interest movement were developed before the peak of the protest over the war (149). See also Jack L. Walker Jr., *Mobilizing Interest Groups in America: Patrons, Professions, and Social Movements* (Ann Arbor, Mich., 1991), 35–40.

40. Brian Balogh, *Chain Reaction: Expert Debate and Public Participation in American Commercial Nuclear Power, 1945–1975* (New York, 1991).

41. See Thomas E. Patterson, *Out of Order* (New York, 1994); and conclusion to Nye, Zelikow, and King, *Why People Don't Trust Government,* 266.

42. Hugh Heclo, "The Sixties' False Dawn: Awakenings, Movements, and Postmodern Policy-Making," in Balogh, *Integrating the Sixties,* 50.

43. Ibid., 52, 58. David Vogel also questions whether Vietnam and Watergate adequately explain the political orientations of the public interest movement, although its suspicion of bureaucratic authority is linked to these traumas. Vogel, *Kindred Strangers,* 149. On the growing divisiveness of politics, see also Dionne, *Why American Hate Politics;* Deborah Tannen, *The Argument Culture: Moving from Debate to Dialogue* (New York, 1998);

Samuel Kernell, *Going Public: New Strategies of Presidential Leadership* (Washington, D.C., 1993); and Benjamin Ginsberg and Martin Shefter, *Politics by Other Means: The Declining Importance of Elections in America* (New York, 1990), 171–78.

44. Louis Galambos, "Paying Up: The Price of the Vietnam War," in Balogh, *Integrating the Sixties,* 171. For a useful chronology of the Cold War, see Anders Stephanson, "The United States," in David Reynolds, ed., *The Origins of the Cold War in Europe: International Perspectives* (New Haven, Conn., 1994), 25.

45. Cerny is quoted in Ernest R. May, "The Evolving Scope of Government," in Nye, Zelikow, and King, *Why People Don't Trust Government,* 52. For a commentary on how the changing status of the national security state contributed to President Clinton's troubles with Special Prosecutor Kenneth Starr, see Brian Balogh, "An Evolving Presidency," *Los Angeles Times,* August 2, 1998.

46. For an interesting meditation on the new basis for shaping personal identities, see May, "Evolving Scope of Government," 53.

47. For an extended discussion of the postwar relationship between state and individual, see the introduction to Balogh, *Integrating the Sixties,* 1–33.

3. Preparing *Not* to Refight the Last War

The author gratefully acknowledges the research assistance of Robert Flynn. Dr. John Carland, Lt. Col. Mark Clodfelter, Dr. Earl Tilford, and Dr. Jack Shulimson provided valuable help in locating sources, and Dr. Edward M. Coffman, Lt. Col. Conrad Crane, Col. Robert Doughty, and Professor Michael Desch read an early draft and offered numerous useful suggestions.

1. Quoted in Guenter Lewy, *America in Vietnam* (New York, 1978), 154.

2. Quoted in William M. Hammond, *Public Affairs: The Military and the Media, 1968–1973* (Washington, D.C., 1996), 371, 373.

3. Powell is quoted in Al Santoli, *Leading the Way: How Vietnam Veterans Rebuilt the U.S. Military: An Oral History* (New York, 1993), 101–2. For excellent general discussions of the breakdown late in the war, see Hammond, *Public Affairs,* 369–99; and for the Marines, Graham Cosmas and Lt. Col. Terrence P. Murray, *U.S. Marines in Vietnam: Vietnamization and Redeployment, 1970–1971* (Washington, D.C., 1986), 343–69.

4. Hammond, *Public Affairs,* 388–92.

5. Jonathan Schell, *Observing the Nixon Years* (New York, 1989), 61. See also George C. Herring, "'Peoples Quite Apart': Americans, South Vietnamese, and the War in Vietnam," *Diplomatic History* 14 (Winter 1990), esp. 16–19.

6. Cosmas and Murray, *Vietnamization,* 353.

7. Quoted in Santoli, *Leading the Way,* 78.

8. Ronald H. Spector, "The Vietnam War and the Army's Self-Image," in John Schlight, ed., *Second Indochina War Symposium: Papers and Commentary* (Washington, D.C., 1986), 175.

9. Loren Baritz, *Backfire: A History of How American Culture Led Us into Vietnam and Made Us Fight the Way We Did* (New York, 1985), 298–300.

10. Interview with Col. Arthur Kelly, Frankfort, Ky., May 1985.

11. *U.S. News & World Report,* June 16, 1975, 45–46.

12. Cosmas and Murray, *Vietnamization,* 362–63.

13. Powell is quoted in Santoli, *Leading the Way,* 101–2. On the persistent difficulties in the Marine Corps, see Thomas E. Ricks, *Making the Corps* (New York, 1997), 136–37.

14. See, for example, Elmo R. Zumwalt Jr., *On Watch: Memoir* (Arlington, Va., 1976), 167–272; and James Kitfield, *Prodigal Soldiers: How the Generation of Officers Born of Vietnam Revolutionized the American Style of War* (New York, 1995), 136–38.

15. Kitfield, *Prodigal Soldiers,* 134–38; Robert K. Griffith Jr., *The U.S. Army's Transition to the All-Volunteer Force, 1968–1974* (Washington, D.C., 1997).

16. "The New Look Army," *Newsweek,* March 28, 1977, 20–21; Kitfield, *Prodigal Soldiers,* 199, 206–7.

17. Lewis Sorley, *Thunderbolt: General Creighton Abrams and the Army of His Times* (New York, 1992), 360–65.

18. Kitfield, *Prodigal Soldiers,* 349–50.

19. Col. Harry G. Summers Jr., *On Strategy II: Critical Analyses of the Gulf War* (New York, 1992), 79.

20. Russell F. Weigley, *The American Way of War* (Bloomington, Ind., 1977), 406–20.

21. Summers, *On Strategy II,* 81–82.

22. Ibid., 83; Edward M. Coffman, "The Course of Military History in

the United States since World War II," *Journal of Military History* 61 (October 1997): 769–70.

23. Kenneth J. Hagan, *This People's Navy: The Making of American Sea Power* (New York, 1991), 376–80, 387.

24. On the rewriting of Army doctrine in the 1970s and 1980s, see Kitfield, *Prodigal Soldiers,* 158–65, 192, 302–3; and Rick Atkinson, *Crusade: The Untold Story of the Persian Gulf War* (Boston, 1993), 252–53.

25. Lt. Col. Conrad Crane, "Avoiding Another Vietnam: The US Army's Response to Defeat in Southeast Asia," unpublished paper in author's possession, 4.

26. Paul Herbert, *Deciding What Has to Be Done: General William E. DePuy and the 1976 Edition of FM 100–5, Operations,* Leavenworth Paper 16 (Fort Leavenworth, Kans., 1988).

27. On the emergence of AirLand doctrine in the 1970s and 1980s, see Kitfield, *Prodigal Soldiers,* 158–65, 192, 302–3; and Atkinson, *Crusade,* 252–53.

28. Harry G. Summers Jr., *On Strategy: A Critical Analysis of the Vietnam War* (Carlisle, Pa., 1981); Crane, "Avoiding Another Vietnam," 12; Conrad Crane, "Playing with Razor Blades: The American Military and *On Strategy,*" unpublished paper in author's possession. Andrew Krepivenich, *The Army and Vietnam* (Baltimore, 1986) is a sharp attack on Summers's thesis and the Army's preoccupation with conventional warfare. Russell Weigley's paper "The Impact of World War II on U.S. Army Doctrine," copy in author's possession, also addresses the Army's fixation with conventional warfare.

29. Mark Clodfelter and John M. Fawcett Jr., "The RMA and Air Force Roles, Missions, and Doctrine," *Parameters,* Summer 1995, 29. This section is based on telephone interviews with Mark Clodfelter and Earl Tilford and on Dennis M. Drew, "Air Theory, Air Force, and Low Intensity Conflict: A Short Journey to Confusion," in Col. Phillip S. Meilinger, ed., *The Paths of Heaven: The Evolution of Airpower Theory* (Maxwell Air Force Bases, Ala., 1997), 321–54. For the most recent debate, see *Air Force Basic Doctrine* (Washington, D.C., 1997); and Clodfelter and Fawcett, "RMA," 22–29.

30. Kitfield, *Prodigal Soldiers,* 162.

31. Santoli, *Leading the Way,* 260–61.

32. Bob Woodward, *The Commanders* (New York, 1991), 129–30; Kitfield, *Prodigal Soldiers,* 192, 310; Romie L. Brownlee and William J. Mullen III, *Changing an Army: An Oral History of General William E. DePuy, USA Retired* (Carlisle Barracks, Pa., 1985).

33. Ricks, *Making the Corps,* 142.

34. Quoted in Ricks, *Making the Corps,* 144. Gray's role is recounted on pp. 137–46. See also Santoli, *Leading the Way,* 137–38, 373; and Atkinson, *Crusade,* 252–53.

35. See, for example, George C. Herring, *LBJ and Vietnam: A Different Kind of War* (Austin, Tex., 1994), esp. chap. 2.

36. Mark Perry, *Four Stars* (Boston, 1989), 338.

37. Ibid., 337.

38. *U.S. News & World Report,* April 22, 1985, 37–38.

39. Kitfield, *Prodigal Soldiers,* 212.

40. *U.S. News & World Report,* April 22, 1985, 37–38; *Time,* November 4, 1985, 4.

41. Richard Armitage, "Vietnam Retrospection," *U.S. Naval Institute Proceedings,* November 1985, 76.

42. Richard Halloran, *To Arm a Nation: Rebuilding America's Endangered Defenses* (New York, 1986), 28.

43. Quoted in David H. Petraeus, "Lessons of History and Lessons of Vietnam," *Parameters* 16 (Autumn 1986): 45.

44. Drew Middleton, "Vietnam and the Military Mind," *New York Times Magazine,* January 10, 1982, 34.

45. Petraeus, "Lessons of History," 43–51; and David H. Petraeus, "Military Influence and the Post-Vietnam Use of Force," *Armed Forces and Society* 15 (Summer 1989): 489–505.

46. Caspar Weinberger, *Fighting for Peace: Seven Critical Years in the Pentagon* (New York, 1990), 159.

47. Ibid., 8–9, 31; the so-called Weinberger rules are on pp. 433–45.

48. George P. Shultz, *Turmoil and Triumph: My Years as Secretary of State* (New York, 1993), 649–541.

49. Colin L. Powell with Joseph E. Persico, *My American Journey* (New York, 1995), 302–3. See also Atkinson, *Crusade,* 122; and Woodward, *Commanders,* 89–90.

50. Quoted in Santoli, *Leading the Way,* 8, 52.

51. Quoted in *New York Times,* January 28, 1991. Atkinson, *Crusade,* and

Woodward, *Commanders,* are full of references to Vietnam by Gulf War political and military leaders.

52. Kitfield, *Prodigal Soldiers,* 334.

53. There were still problems, of course. National Security Adviser Brent Scowcroft and JCS chairman Powell interfered more than Schwarzkopf would have liked. But the major problems developed between Schwarzkopf and his Army commanders, in part the result of the former's domineering personality and arbitrary treatment of his subordinates, in part because of the concern, deeply ingrained in the commanders as a result of Vietnam, to minimize casualties among their forces. See Richard Swain, *"Lucky War": Third Army in Desert Storm* (Fort Leavenworth, Kans., 1994), 333–38.

54. *Lexington Herald-Leader,* January 27, 1991.

55. *New York Times,* February 24, 1991.

56. Quoted in Santoli, *Leading the Way,* 421.

57. This view is advanced in Kitfield, *Prodigal Soldiers;* Atkinson, *Crusade;* and Santoli, *Leading the Way.*

58. Crane, "Avoiding Another Vietnam," 13–14, 2; see also Ricks, *Making the Corps,* 178, 180.

59. For a scathing critique of the performance of the military and the media in the Gulf War, see John R. MacArthur, *Second Front: Censorship and Propaganda in the Gulf War* (New York, 1992).

60. Richard H. Kohn, "Out of Control—The Crisis in Civil-Military Relations," *The National Interest* 35 (Spring 1994): 3–17.

61. Powell, *My American Journey,* 149.

62. Russell F. Weigley, "The American Military and the Principle of Civilian Control from McClellan to Powell," *Journal of Military History* 57 (October 1993): 27–29.

63. Ibid., 12; Roger Cohen, "After the Vultures: Holbrooke's Bosnia Peace Came Too Late," *Foreign Affairs,* May/June 1998, 109. The United States spent millions of dollars developing plans and training troops to capture two major war criminals, but top military leaders rejected them because they were deemed too risky. See *New York Times,* July 26, 1998.

64. Ricks, *Making the Corps,* 275. See also Robert D. Kaplan, "Fort Leavenworth and the Eclipse of Nationhood," *Atlantic Monthly,* September 1996, 78, which refers to the military as a "self-interested bureaucracy with the power of negotiation."

65. Jeffrey Record, paper presented at conference on the Vietnam War and the Gulf War, Georgia Institute of Technology, Atlanta, February 1991. On complications from the Bosnia operation, see *Lexington Herald-Leader,* May 25, 1998.

66. See *Lexington Herald-Leader,* June ll, 1998; September 26, 28, 1998.

67. Clarence Page, column in *Lexington Herald-Leader,* November 18, 1997.

68. Ricks, *Making the Corps,* 20. See also Arnold R. Isaacs, *Vietnam Shadows: The War, Its Ghosts, and Its Legacy* (Baltimore, 1997), 41–42, 70–71; and Ole R. Holsti, "A Wide Gap between the Military and Civilian Society? Some Evidence, 1976–1996," John M. Olin Institute for Strategic Studies, Project on US Post Cold War Civil-Military Relations, Working Papers No. 13 (October 1997); and Thomas R. Ricks, "The Widening Gap between the Military and Society," *Atlantic Monthly* 280 (July 1997): 67–78.

69. Kohn, "Out of Control," 15–17.

70. Ricks, *Making the Corps,* 285.

4. Revolutionary Heroism and Politics in Postwar Vietnam

1. Nguyen Khac Vien, "Confucianism and Marxism," in David Marr and Jayne Werner, eds., *Tradition and Revolution in Vietnam* (Berkeley, 1974), 47.

2. *May van de tong ket chien tranh va viet lich su quan su* [Selected issues related to the conclusions and the writing of the military history of the war] (Hanoi, 1987). See also Pham van Dong, "Phat huy chu nghia anh hung cach mang, day manh su nghiep chong My, cuu nuoc den thang loi hoan toan" [Promote revolutionary heroism, strengthen the anti-U.S. resistance war for national salvation of the fatherland to lead to complete victory], *Hoc Tap* 13 (January 1967): 17–20.

3. William Duiker, *Vietnam: Revolution in Transition,* 2d ed. (Boulder, Colo., 1995), 123.

4. Frances FitzGerald, *Fire in the Lake: The Vietnamese and the Americans in Vietnam* (New York, 1972), 512.

5. Ho Chi Minh was founder of the Vietnamese Communist Party and its president from 1929 to 1969. The Trung sisters are credited with leading Vietnam's first revolution against China in A.D. 40. Le Loi is one of the most celebrated Vietnamese leaders; he led the fifteenth-century resistance

movement against the Chinese occupation armies of the Ming dynasty. Nguyen Hue led the peasant uprising known as the Tay Son Rebellion (1771–88).

6. Vuong Thanh, "The Hero Mothers of Vietnam," *Vietnam Courier* 172 (December 15–21, 1996): 2.

7. Quoted in Stanley Karnow, *Vietnam: A History* (New York, 1983), 9.

8. William Duiker, *Sacred War: Nationalism and Revolution in a Divided Vietnam* (New York, 1995), 261.

9. According to William Duiker, the VCP had little choice. Duiker argues that there were three essential reasons for the swift action by Hanoi. The long and costly war had seriously depleted the number of trained and dedicated cadres in the south. As a result, Hanoi would have to send replacements from the north. For a variety of reasons, this was far easier to do in a united Vietnam. Furthermore, the economy, in a shambles because of the war, would have to be nursed back to health. The management of this economy, Duiker suggests, was easier to control by mechanisms already established in Hanoi. Party leaders, therefore, saw an economic imperative in an expeditious reunification. Finally, northern Party leaders correctly feared action by southern dissidents. According to Duiker, VCP officials had concluded by mid-1975 that "the longer the delay in unification, the more potential obstacles could be expected to arise." See Duiker, *Vietnam: Revolution in Transition,* 109–10.

10. Radio Hanoi, broadcast in Vietnamese, 1400 GMT, November 15, 1975.

11. *Nhan Dan,* November 29, 1975.

12. *Far Eastern Economic Review,* December 5, 1975, 23.

13. Author interview with Nguyen Co Thach, former foreign minister of the Socialist Republic of Vietnam, Hanoi, June 1997.

14. Author interview with former VCP official who requested anonymity, Hanoi, March 1996. In all subsequent citations of author interviews in which the interviewee is not named, that person requested anonymity.

15. *Third National Congress of the Viet Nam Workers' Party, Documents* (Hanoi, 1960), 1:252.

16. Alastair Iain Johnson, *Cultural Realism: Strategic Culture and Grand Strategy in Chinese History* (Princeton, N.J., 1996), i.

17. Author interview with former Political Bureau member, Hanoi, June 1997.

18. Author interview with Tran Quang Co, Hanoi, November 1995.

19. Author interview with Luu Van Loi, former Foreign Ministry official, Hanoi, February 1998.

20. Author interview with Nguyen Co Thach, Hanoi, November 1995.

21. Author interview with former Central Committee member, Hanoi, March 1996.

22. Viet Nam News Agency, March 23, 1987.

23. Author interview with former Central Committee member, Hanoi, February 1998.

24. Truong Nhu Tang, *A Viet Cong Memoir: An Inside Account of the Vietnam War and Its Aftermath* (New York, 1985), 264–65.

25. Author interview with former VCP official, Hanoi, February 1998.

26. Author interview with former VCP official, Hanoi, June 1997.

27. Viet Nam News Agency, March 4, 1982.

28. Gareth Porter, *Vietnam: The Politics of Bureaucratic Socialism* (Ithaca, N.Y., 1993), 107.

29. Carlyle A. Thayer, "Renovation and Vietnamese Society: The Changing Roles of Government and Administration," paper presented to Conference on Viet Nam's Economic Renovation, convened by the Research School of Pacific Studies, Australian National University, Canberra, September 19–21, 1990. See also Gareth Porter, "The Politics of Renovation in Viet Nam," *Problems of Communism* 39 (May–June 1990): 80–85.

30. Thayer, "Renovation and Vietnamese Society."

31. Author interview with Luu Van Loi, Hanoi, February 1998.

32. Author interview with former Foreign Ministry official, Hanoi, February 1998.

33. The mandate of heaven was the right to rule by heaven's will. In traditional Vietnam, the mandarins were the only people concerned with affairs of state. It was their responsibility, therefore, to understand the will of heaven and lead accordingly. In times of great uncertainty, however, the peasants did concern themselves with political life. When they sensed that the mandate of heaven had changed, they often pressed for dramatic change.

34. Author interview with Le Phuong, Hoi An, March 1996.

35. Bui Tin, *From Cadre to Exile: The Memoirs of a North Vietnamese Journalist* (Chiang Mai, 1995), 103.

36. Author interview with former VCP official, Hanoi, November 1995.

37. Bui Tin, *From Cadre to Exile,* 103.

38. Author interview with former VCP official, Hanoi, February 1998.

39. Quoted in Bui Tin, *From Cadre to Exile,* 139.

40. Porter, *Vietnam: The Politics of Bureaucratic Socialism,* 154.

41. Motoo Furuta, "The Sixth Party Congress in the History of Vietnamese Communism," in Tadashi Mio, ed., *International Relations around Indochina* (Tokyo, 1988), 24.

42. *New York Times,* September 20, 1989.

43. Duiker, *Vietnam: Revolution in Transition,* 119. See also Porter, *Vietnam: The Politics of Bureaucratic Socialism,* 104.

44. Author interview with former VCP official, Hanoi, May 1997.

45. Author interview with former VCP official, Hanoi, June 1997.

46. Author interview with former Central Committee member, Hanoi, January 1997.

47. Thayer, "Renovation and Vietnamese Society."

48. Author interview with former university professor, Ho Chi Minh City, March 1996.

49. Author interview with former VCP official, Hanoi, March 1996.

50. Author interview with former VCP official, Hanoi, November 1995.

51. Author interview with student, Hue, March 1996.

52. Author interview with student, Hanoi, February 1998.

53. Quoted in Duiker, *Vietnam: Revolution in Transition,* 120.

54. Bui Tin, *From Cadre to Exile,* viii.

55. Ibid. See also Bui Tin, *Following Ho Chi Minh: Memoirs of a North Vietnamese Colonel,* trans. Judy Stowe and Do Van (London, 1994; published in the United States by University of Hawaii Press, 1995).

56. Author interview with Dan Duffy, Hanoi, March 1996. See also Dan Duffy, ed., *North Viet Nam Now: Fiction and Essays from Ha Noi* (New Haven, Conn., 1996).

57. Jonathan Mirsky, "No Trumpets, No Drums," *New York Review of Books,* September 21, 1995, 60.

58. Bao Ninh, *The Sorrow of War: A Novel of North Vietnam* (New York, 1993).

59. Duong Thu Huong, *Paradise of the Blind* [*Nhung Thien Duong Mu*], trans. Phan Huy Duong and Nina McPherson (New York, 1993).

60. Duong Thu Huong, *Novel without a Name* [*Tieu Thuyet Vo De*], trans. Phan Huy Duong and Nina McPherson (New York, 1995).

61. George McT. Kahin and John Lewis, *The United States in Vietnam: An Analysis in Depth of the History of America's Involvement in Vietnam* (New York, 1967), 253.

62. Author interview with Nguyen Le, National University student, Ho Chi Minh City, March 1996.

63. Author interview with Nguyen Van Bo, National University student, Ho Chi Minh City, March 1996.

64. Author interview with Haiphong resident, Hanoi, February 1996.

65. Author interview with student, Hanoi, January 1997.

66. Carlyle A. Thayer, "Vietnam Country Report, 1996," <http://www.coombs.anu.edu.au>.

67. Dennis Rockstroh, "The Hidden Horror of Vietnam's Camps," *San Jose Mercury News,* October 11, 1987. See also Duiker, *Sacred War,* 266.

68. Author interview with former university professor, Hanoi, January 1997.

69. Author interview with National University student, Hanoi, January 1997.

70. Ly Thai Bung, "Who Will Replace Le Duc Anh?" Viet Nam News Agency, January 7, 1997.

5. Reflections on War in the Twenty-first Century

1. Carnegie Commission on Preventing Deadly Conflict, Carnegie Corporation, *Preventing Deadly Conflict, Final Report* (New York, December 1997), xii.

2. *New York Times,* December 31, 1989.

3. Henry Kissinger, *Diplomacy* (New York, 1994), 805.

4. Carl Kaysen, "Is War Obsolete?" *International Security* 14, no. 4 (Spring 1990): 63.

5. I have included in my concept of "collective security" elements of what Janne Nolan refers to as "Cooperative Security." Nolan states that "one strategy does not preclude the other and both are, in fact, mutually reinforcing." Janne E. Nolan, ed., *Global Engagement: Cooperation and Security in the Twenty-first Century* (Washington, D.C., 1994), 5.

6. *New York Times,* September 28, 1993.

7. *Washington Post,* June 11, 1994.

8. George F. Kennan, "NATO: A Fateful Error," *New York Times*, February 5, 1997.

9. Ernest R. May and Philip D. Zelikow, *The Kennedy Tapes: Inside the White House during the Cuban Missile Crisis* (Cambridge, Mass., 1997).

10. Aleksandr V. Fursenko and Timothy Naftali, *"One Hell of a Gamble": Khrushchev, Castro, and Kennedy, 1958–1964* (New York, 1997).

11. General Gribkov elaborated on these points at a meeting at the Woodrow Wilson International Center for Scholars, Washington, D.C., on April 5, 1994.

12. See Anatoly Dokochaev, "Afterword to Sensational 100 Day Nuclear Cruise," *Krasnaya Zvezda*, November 6, 1992; and V. Badurikin interview with Dimitri Volkogonov in "Operation Anadry," *Trud*, October 27, 1992.

13. Both the Canberra Commission and the Carnegie Commission came to the same conclusion. Using almost identical words, they state: "The position that large numbers of nuclear weapons can be retained in perpetuity and never used—accidentally or by decision—defies credibility." *Report of the Canberra Commission on the Elimination of Nuclear Weapons* (Canberra, 1996), 22; Carnegie Commission on Preventing Deadly Conflict, *Preventing Deadly Conflict*, 70.

14. This statement was endorsed by the National Academy of Sciences in 1991 in a report signed by eighteen security experts, including former Air Force Chief of Staff David C. Jones (*The Future of the U.S.-Soviet Nuclear Relationship* [Washington, D.C.: National Academy Press, 1991], 3); by the Stimson Center's Panel on Nuclear Forces, chaired by General Andrew Goodpaster (*An Evolving Nuclear Posture* [Washington, D.C., December 1995], 15); and by the *Report of the Canberra Commission on the Elimination of Nuclear Weapons*, 18.

15. I recognize, of course, that the abolition of nuclear weapons would not be possible without development of an adequate verification system. Are acceptable verification regimes feasible? The decisive point of whether verification is adequate for complete elimination (as opposed to reductions to a level of, say, one hundred warheads) is not likely to be resolved for some time. In the end, comparative risks must be evaluated. The Canberra Commission, which also recommended abolition, concluded that the risk of use of the weapons far exceeds the risks associated with whatever nuclear force a cheating state could assemble before it was exposed.

16. See John J. Fialka and Frederick Kemps, "U.S. Welcomes Soviet Arms Plan, but Dismissed Pact as Propaganda," *Wall Street Journal,* January 17, 1986.

17. See Secretary of Defense William Perry's statement to the Stimson Center, September 20, 1994; and Department of Defense briefing, September 22, 1994.

18. McGeorge Bundy, William J. Crowe Jr., and Sidney O. Drell, *Reducing Nuclear Danger: The Road Away from the Brink* (New York, 1993), 100.

19. Stimson Center, *An Evolving Nuclear Posture.*

20. *Report of the Canberra Commission on the Elimination of Nuclear Weapons*, 7.

21. National Academy Press, Washington, D.C., 1997, 59, 80.

22. See Solly Zuckerman, *Nuclear Illusion and Reality* (New York, 1982), 70; and *Sunday Times* (London), February 21, 1982.

23. Henry Kissinger, "NATO Defense and the Soviet Threat," *Survival,* November–December 1979, 266.

24. Helmut Schmidt, BBC Radio interview with Stuart Simon, July 16, 1987.

25. Larry Welch to Adam Scheinman, March 21, 1994.

26. *Boston Globe,* July 16, 1994.

27. Robert S. McNamara, "The Military Role of Nuclear Weapons," *Foreign Affairs,* Fall 1983, 79.

28. "De-alerting Strategic Nuclear Forces," a preliminary draft of a study of nuclear forces presented by Bruce G. Blair on January 29, 1998, to the Independent Task Force on Reducing the Risk of Nuclear War, Brookings Institution.

Contributors

Brian Balogh is Associate Professor of History at the University of Virginia. He is the author of *Chain Reaction: Expert Debate and Public Participation in American Commercial Nuclear Power, 1945–1975* and editor of *Integrating the Sixties: The Origins, Structures, and Legitimacy of Public Policy in a Turbulent Decade.* He recently served as a fellow at the Woodrow Wilson International Center for Scholars.

Robert K. Brigham is Associate Professor of History at Vassar College. A specialist in Vietnamese history and culture, he is the author of *Guerrilla Diplomacy: The NLF's Foreign Relations and the Viet Nam War.* He is completing a study of the Army of the Republic of Vietnam (ARVN) and recently held a research fellowship from the Smith Richardson Foundation.

George C. Herring is Alumni Professor of History at the University of Kentucky. He is the author of many books, articles, and essays, including *The Secret Diplomacy of the Vietnam War: The Negotiating Volumes of the Pentagon Papers; LBJ and Vietnam: A Different Kind of War;* and *America's Longest War: The United States and Vietnam, 1950–1975.* A former Guggenheim Fellow and Visiting Fulbright Scholar in New Zealand, he is a past president of the Society for Historians of American Foreign Relations.

Robert S. McNamara served as president of the Ford Motor Company from 1960 to 1961, as Secretary of Defense from 1961 to 1968, and as president of the World Bank from 1968 to 1981. He is the author of *Blundering into Disaster: Surviving the First Century of the Nuclear Age;* with Brian VanDeMark, *In Retrospect: The Tragedy and Lessons of Vietnam;* and *Argument Without End: In Search of Answers to the Vietnam Tragedy.*

Charles E. Neu is Professor of History and Chair, Department of History, Brown University. He is the author of *An Uncertain Friendship: Theodore Roosevelt and Japan, 1901–1909* and *The Troubled Encounter: The United States and Japan;* and co-editor of *The Wilson Era: Essays in Honor of Arthur S. Link.* He has held fellowships from the Guggenheim Foundation and the National Endowment for the Humanities.

Index

Library of Congress Cataloging-in-Publication Data

After Vietnam : legacies of a lost war / edited by Charles E.
Neu.

p. cm.

Includes bibliographical references and index.

ISBN 0-8018-6327-9 (hardcover : alk. paper)—ISBN 0-
8018-6332-5 (alk. paper)

1. Vietnamese Conflict, 1961–1975—United States. 2.
Vietnamese Conflict, 1961–1975—Influence. 3. United
States—History—1969– 4. Vietnam—History—1975–
I. Neu, Charles E.

DS558 .A37 2000
959.704'3373—dc21 99-053818